FISH TALES
A collection of true angling stories

FISH TALES

A COLLECTION OF TRUE ANGLING STORIES

EDITED BY
BILLEE CHAPMAN PINCHER

Illustrations
by
Ben Perkins

UNWIN

HYMAN

London   Sydney   Wellington

First published in Great Britain by Unwin Hyman, an imprint of Unwin Hyman Limited, 1989

UNWIN HYMAN LIMITED
15/17 Broadwick Street, London W1V 1FP

Allen & Unwin Australia Pty Ltd
8 Napier Street, North Sydney, NSW 2060, Australia

Allen & Unwin New Zealand with the Port Nicholson Press
Compusales Building, 75 Ghuznee Street, Wellington, New Zealand

British Library Cataloguing in Publication Data

Pincher, Billee Chapman
Fish tales: a collection of true angling stories.
1. Fishing. Anecdotes, facetiae, satire, etc
I. Title
799.1'2
ISBN 004 440448 4

Typeset in 11.5 on 13.5 Sabon
Printed in Great Britain at the University Press, Cambridge

CONTENTS

List of Illustrations	vi
List of Contributors	vii
Hooked!	1
Fishy Business	77
Intruders	123
The Nineteenth Pool	179

ILLUSTRATIONS

1 An Accommodating Salmon   7
2 Green Mamba!   26
3 'Get it!'   42
4 'Mercy, aye! The urn and my hat's awa!'   68
5 'It's a bloody kelt!'   73
6 So *That's* How it's Done!   80
7 A Cast too Far   96
8 Fisherman's Protest   103
9 'I have no faith in my leader!'   108
10 Not in the Fly Box – or Strictly According
   to Skues   119
11 A Rapist!   130
12 The Watcher in the Wood   133
13 Salmon in the Brambles   155
14 Hardening the Horse's legs   174
15 Keeping the Rod well up   177
16 Phantom Fox   222

CONTRIBUTORS

Major-General Sir
  John Acland
Peter Adam
Richard Adams
Bernard Aldrich
Ian Anderson
The Duke of Atholl
David Barr
Tony Barron
Richie Benaud
Barry Black
Jack Block
Anthony Bone
Lord Brabourne
John Bridgeman
Peter Bridgeman
Alan Bristow
Captain George
  Brodrick
Gary Brooker
Lord Jock Bruce-
  Gardyne
Mary Carswell
Cavaliere del
  Lavoro Massimo
  Coen
Billee Chapman
  Pincher
Harry Chapman
  Pincher
Michael Clark

Jack Coates
The Earl of
  Dalhousie
Jan Eckman
Alan Elliot
Sir Eric Faulkner
The Duke of Fife
Bob Findlay
Vic Foot
Lord Forte
Major Derek Foster
John Fowles
Ed Gardyne
Jason Garrett
Sir Donald Gosling
Mrs William Govett
Jane Hall
Richard Hall
Derek Hallum
Max Hastings
Barbara Hawkins
Joan Hirsch
Lord Home of the
  Hirsel
Sir Michael
  Hordern
Ted Hughes
Peter Hutley
Tony Ingram
Air Vice-Marshal
  Johnnie Johnson

Sir Geoffrey
  Johnson-Smith
Professor R. V.
  Jones
Ernest Juer
Peter Katin
The Earl of Kimberley
Sir Hector Laing
Robert Lamphere
Nicole Law
Alan Lawrence
Admiral of the Fleet Sir
  Henry Leach
Lord Mason
Colonel I. H.
  McCausland
George Melly
Professor Harry
  Messel
Sir Denis Mountain
Sam Nickerson
Charles Oliver-
  Bellasis
The Hon. Colin
  Orr-Ewing
Tommy Parrington
Tony Pawson
The Earl of
  Pembroke
Boy Pilkington
Anthony Prender-
  gast
Ken Robinson
Ginger Rogers
John Sautelle
Frank Sawyer
Colonel Henry
  Segal

Lord Sieff
Sir Thomas Sopwith
Lady Sopwith
Peter Spence
Major Anthony
  Stansfeld
The Rt Hon. David Steel,
  MP
Anthony Strick
David Sussman
General Sir David
  Thorne
Viscount Thurso
Roger de Vere
Malcolm Wallop
Gerald Ward
Colonel Jackie
  Ward
Veronica Weld-
  Blundell
The Duke of Wellington
Dermot Wilson
Shirley E. Woods

HOOKED!

'A fisherman's tale' has become an established phrase, in many languages, for a tall story, a greatly exaggerated account or an outright lie. There is even a rhyme which poses the question 'Are all fishermen liars or do all liars fish?' The 'one that got away' is a natural and inevitable fount of exaggeration but the basic truth is that quite extraordinary things do happen in fishing and that, I believe, is the real reason why angling has generated more strange stories than any other sport, even golf, and will continue to do so. As that wonderful old sportsman Sir Thomas Sopwith remarked when I told him I was going to take up fishing, some twenty-five years ago, 'It's the one sport where there are no rules. Anything can happen and it usually does.'

His prediction has proved to be so accurate in my own experience that I decided to collect as many true tall tales as I could from distinguished people, who would not lend their names to them unless they were entirely authentic. I present a selection of them in this book. I have also collected stories from gillies, some of whom are notorious leg pullers. I have included only those which I know to be true from checking with other people.

The commonest fishing tale is of the duffer, or the small child with a bent pin, who catches fish when the experts fail. This almost happened to me.

When I married Harry Chapman Pincher I quickly realised that if I was not to become a fishing and shooting widow I had better come to terms with both. Shooting posed no problem as, being of country origin, I was used to going out with the Guns and my husband had springer spaniels which I could use for picking up. Fishing was new to me but I was prepared to have a try.

My first lesson was on the lawn prior to a salmon fishing trip to Ireland. My husband showed me how to cast a spinning bait, which he was able to do with great accuracy, placing the bait within a few inches of a saucer at long distances. When I tried the bait went all over the place and the line was soon in a fearful mess. Not renowned for his patience, my husband simply said 'Go on practising and do a little every day when I am at the office' and left me to it.

I resolved my problem by finding the name of a fishing instructor at Virginia Water and taking lessons surreptitiously for three weeks. Shortly before we were due to leave for Ireland my husband asked me to show him how I had progressed with my lawn practice and was astounded by the result. 'You must be a natural fisher,' he concluded. I did not enlighten him.

My pride and prowess were short-lived, however, once I began in earnest on the River Slaney, fishing against a wind. The Irish gillie was appalled at my succession of overruns and, after disentangling the third, left me with the comment 'I'll just be over the hill to see how your husband is getting on.'

'What happens if I get a fish?'

'Just shout and wave a handkerchief.'

He had barely disappeared when I felt a snap at the bait and the line began to move out into the strong current. Nobody had told me how to play a fish, or if they had I had forgotten it. I shouted myself hoarse and waved the handkerchief when I could but nobody came. Fortunately, the salmon stopped and lay on the bottom and I just stood there, keeping my rod point up, for about fifteen minutes and praying that the gillie would come.

Harry and the gillie suddenly came into view and broke into a run as they heard my cry 'I've got a fish!' My husband had one look at the static line and commented, 'You must be on the bottom.' He took the rod, put strain on the line and the fish shot away. Scared that I would lose my first salmon, I wanted him to play it but he handed me the rod and insisted that I finish the job. 'What if I lose it?' I asked.

'It won't be the last you'll lose, madam,' was all the response I got from the gillie.

Under instruction we soon had the fish – a 13-pounder – on the bank and from that moment I knew that I was hooked myself.

A few weeks later, back at our home in Surrey, my husband returned from a day's trout fishing with Sir Thomas Sopwith on the Test, near Stockbridge, where the river keeper for many years had been an elderly man called Ted Hill 'You will be sorry to hear that Ted Hill dropped dead the other day,' he said. 'He died playing a salmon, lower down the Test at Nursling.'

My response was immediate. 'Did they get the fish?'

It was then that my husband knew that I was hooked on fishing.

Barbara Hawkins also became dedicated to the sport, despite the restrictions imposed at the beginning of her angling career.

Shortly after I had started to fish, many years ago, I was invited to share a rod with Jimmy Cadman, a well-known sportsman best remembered by the hunting and shooting fraternity, as he had been Chairman of the North Staffs hunt for many years and also had the grouse-shooting on Blubberhouse Moor. He had suffered so many fractures of a collar-bone that the last major repair had left it unfit for heavy duty. Hence my invitation to share the rod on the Cambus O'May beat of the Dee.

I was very excited and kept asking how we would work out the sharing. He had already worked out the answer – my language was so notoriously bad that he said he would try to improve it by means of a penalty system. I was to be allowed one b. . . . . and one f. . . and would then have to come out of the pool and permit him to take over.

On the Monday morning I was first to start – on the best pool of the beat. Shaking with nerves and excitement, for I really was a beginner, I strode down the bank only to trip over my wading stick. Out came the first b. . . . . .

'One gone!' cried Jimmy.

I carried on trying to get my line out in a fair wind and produced a deafening crack as the fly disappeared. Out came the inevitable f... followed by a shriek of delight from Jimmy. 'Out you come, my girl, and may that be a lesson to you.'

Out I had to come without my fly even touching the water, and I had to sit and watch Jimmy quietly fish down for only a few yards before producing a lovely salmon.

I would like to say that this experience had a dramatic effect on my language and, indeed, I did manage to button up my mouth for that week but I fear it had no lasting influence.

———————————————

I was lucky to catch a salmon on my first day but some have done it with their first cast, as witness this story by **Sir Thomas Sopwith**, the aviation pioneer and internationally renowned sportsman.

Many years ago a non-fishing relative of mine was staying with me at Lochmore. He would listen with mild amusement and a certain amount of astonishment to the fishing conversation and tall stories at the end of every day's sport. After a few days of this he decided to find out for himself what this fishing was all about. So he armed himself with a rod and, accompanied by a gillie, went out in a boat to try his luck in Loch Stack.

After a few minutes' instruction from the gillie our tyro started to fish. With his first cast he got into a sizeable and very athletic salmon, which leapt out of the water straight into the boat and, indeed, full-toss onto the fisherman's lap.

I hoped that the incident would trigger off a lifelong devotion to angling but it did not. Presumably he thought it was all too easy!

7

That was certainly the view of a dear friend of mine, whose one and only fishing experience was recalled for me by her husband, **Lord Forte**, the founder of the world-wide hotel and catering organization.

Years ago, I was salmon fishing on Lake Beltra, in County Mayo, and had managed to persuade my wife, Irene, who was new to fishing, to accompany me in the boat in the hope that she might get interested. I was trolling with a long line and a large plug and, sensing that Irene was bored, I put the rod into her hands saying, 'If anything takes you'll feel a thump and then the fish will take off.'

Her immediate response was to say, 'I think I can feel something now.'

'No,' I replied, patiently. 'That's just the plug working. When it's a fish you won't just think it's a fish. You'll know, because the rod will bend, the reel will screech and the salmon will probably jump out of the water.'

'I still think I can feel something,' my wife insisted.

Wearily I took the rod and tightened, and sure enough she was into a fish.

'Well done!' I declared, putting the rod back in her hands and feeling convinced that she would be hooked on salmon fishing. 'Just reel it in slowly and as soon as it starts to run let it go.'

I watched, keen to see her face when the fireworks started, but she just kept on reeling and the fish just kept on coming. In no time at all I saw its head poke out of the water, completely beaten, and I gaffed it.

My wife looked at me as much as to say, 'Is that all there is to it? Where's the fun? There's nothing to it. It's too easy.'

The fish was fresh and weighed about 12 pounds and I could not understand what had happened until I began to take the bait out of its mouth, when I saw that it was hooked through both lips. From the moment it had taken the bait it had been unable to breathe and the poor creature had had no energy to fight.

I did my best to explain this but the magic moment had passed. My wife had decided that salmon fishing was too tame for her. She never fished again.

Of several fish-on-the-first-cast stories which have come my way, perhaps that supplied by my neighbour, **Alan Elliot**, a Wiltshire businessman, is among the most remarkable.

Fishing the Ash Tree pool on the Kinnaird beat of the Tay with a Devon minnow in September 1988, Mrs Phillipa Chetwode hooked and landed a 10-pound salmon with the first cast she had ever made. Had the river been full of fish the feat might not have seemed so remarkable, but they were so scarce that six of us caught only six fish for the whole week.

The odds against achieving that feat must be high but there was another factor which made them astronomical. Phillipa's husband, Christopher, had brought off exactly the same coup nineteen years previously. Fishing the Wye, he too had hooked a salmon with the first cast he had ever made and had landed it – a fish of some twenty pounds.

Sadly there are many whose experience on their first day's fishing sours them for life. I am indebted to **Roger de Vere**, the distinguished gynaecologist, for the following true story.

The outstanding surgeon Sir Stanford Cade always overworked and his colleagues tried very hard to interest him in fishing as a means of getting him away from the operating theatre. They eventually succeeded in taking him down to fish for salmon on the River Torridge in Devon, where they stayed at a hotel in Torrington. Sadly, during the course of the first morning, Sir Stanford fell in and returned alone to the hotel, where he removed all his clothes and found that his wallet, which was generously filled with £5 notes, was soaked through.

While clad only in a small towel, he busied himself drying out the notes by sticking them on the wall and rang for the maid to bring him some tea. She opened the door, took one look at him, and ran screaming downstairs to the manager, who asked her what was wrong. 'I think the gentleman in Number 25 has gone mad,' she cried. 'He's rushing around stark naked, papering the walls with £5 notes!'

———————————→●←———————————

I understand that Sir Stanford did not try again but others who have had an unhappy initiation have persevered and, ultimately, found fishing to be a perfect relaxation from intellectual and physical endeavour. Such an angler is **Peter Katin**, the celebrated concert pianist.

Inveigled by a friend into trying my hand at sea fishing, I was induced to go with him to Rye Harbour, where, we had been told, once the tide was in one merely had to throw out the line to secure a choice of fine fish for the table.

So, after deciding what we would be having for the following day's dinner, we set out in my car in the dark for the spot in question and drove towards the shingle, having failed, because of the high wind, to hear precisely what the voice in the little customs shed had shouted at us. We realised what it must have been when we stuck in the shingle.

After bravely tackling the situation unaided for more than an hour we sheepishly cast around for help, but Rye Harbour at midnight is not the best place to find it and the owner of the warning voice had long disappeared. Eventually we found the harbour-master's house and he, very obligingly, got out of his bed and lumbered to the rescue, armed with a long pole. 'People do this all the time,' he explained encouragingly.

By 2.30 a.m. the car was freed and removed at speed to a safer spot where we speedily prepared our tackle. We marched with renewed confidence to the harbour but had not taken into account the rather well-known fact that once the tide has come in it will start going out again. The confidence evaporated as we despairingly cast our lines into what seemed like every bit of six inches of water.

However, luck did not entirely desert us. Our respective hooks, which seemed to have a life of their own, decided on a submarine meeting. Momentarily this raised the hopes of both of us as we pulled on each other's lines, and they were duly fulfilled. In the course of the to-ing and fro-ing, the hooks became embedded in the few soft parts of a very large crab.

Apart from the change of menu, we quite enjoyed our dinner the following evening. And my interest in fishing remained alive.

———————— >●< ————————

So did that of **John Bridgeman**, a farmer-landowner, following this sad boyhood experience.

As a small boy intent on catching my first trout, I was fishing in the Brunton Burn where it flowed through a mature sycamore wood not far from my home, Falloden, in Northumberland. As I remember it, conditions were far from ideal for fishing with a worm as the water was too clear, and this meant that I had to make a stealthy and rather painful crawl through the nettles along the bank in order to spot the trout before they saw me. However, I accomplished this and succeeded in gently lowering a worm into the water a few feet upstream of the unsuspecting quarry.

To my great excitement I saw a trout take the worm and, simultaneously, felt, for the very first time, the thrilling sensation of having a fish on the end of my line. The excitement got the better of me and I struck with such force that the unfortunate trout described a parabola as it flew through the air and landed on the bank behind me.

Alas, triumph was all too quickly followed by disaster, for somewhere high above my head the hook and the trout parted company and when I turned to seize my prize it was to see it disappearing, not back into the water, which must have happened many times, but deep down a rabbit hole, which must be very rare.

It was a disconsolate little boy who arrived home late for lunch and my elder brother and sister did not help by their unwillingness to accept that I had ever caught a fish without having one to prove it.

That same brother and sister should have known better because, some years earlier, when they were only six and seven respectively, they too had seen a similar disaster follow closely on their moment of triumph.

The year was 1939 and the place was a fishing lodge called Elverhoï on the River Driva, then undisputedly one of the finest salmon rivers in Norway. The old fishing book records catches dating back to those of Lord Leicester in 1857, and our own family records start a century ago, in 1888, when the property was bought by my uncle. Many of the photographs, old and recent, show a huge granite slab which lies a few yards from the house and on which fishermen at Elverhoi have proudly laid their catches.

One photograph shows six salmon averaging 22 pounds caught by my father before breakfast on 20

June 1921. In 1938 another photograph shows my father sitting on the same stone with Lord Stair and his huge 61-pound salmon. Between them my father, my mother and Lord Stair laid fourteen salmon totalling 297 pounds on the stone that day.

But of all the photographs of proud fishermen standing beside their catches laid out on this great granite slab there is not one which shows two prouder or happier faces than those of my brother and sister kneeling behind their catch of nine minnows. What is not recorded, however, is that while they were in at lunch a cat came and ate the lot, so that the smiles turned to tears and sadness shortly after.

———————————⊃o⊂———————————

That expert angler **Dermot Wilson** has recalled for me someone who seems to have been the ultimate in taking angling adversity on the chin.

I had a friend called Alan. He is now no longer with us but he happened to be the greatest proponent I ever knew of the adage that no true fisherman has to catch fish to enjoy fishing. Sometimes I wonder whether he didn't carry it a little far. He was a mad-keen salmon fisher and for the five seasons before he died he fished every Friday on a famous beat of the Hampshire Avon. In all those five years he never caught one salmon. Nor, if I remember rightly, had he ever caught one anywhere else.

Naturally enough, he was persistently asked by well-meaning friends why he kept on flailing away every Friday, wet or fine, when he never caught anything. His invariable answer was nothing if not dignified – 'I have always maintained that there are many worse ways of spending a Friday afternoon than not catching a salmon.'

What is at the root of such determination? Faith? Hope? It can be sheer logic, according to an experience which befell my husband.

Below the Bavarian Alps, in sight of Zugspitz's frosty summit, curls a comma-shaped lake which, when I saw it in 1949, was heavily stocked with trout. I was visiting an American forces recreation centre which had been set up nearby and as I ambled along the shore I heard mighty splashes which sent my fisherman's blood coursing. I raced round a bend expecting to see five-pounders hurling themselves into the crisp air for the sheer joy of living, but what I saw was nothing more streamlined than a cigar-chewing GI, looking just like whoever is the fat one of Abbott and Costello and whirling a spinning rod with the energy of a Highlander throwing the hammer.

The sight of his khaki form standing high on a rock, with coils of tangled line draped round his neck, impelled me to help this obvious beginner in distress. 'You will never do any good up there,' I called helpfully. 'Trout have exceptionally keen eyesight.'

He moved his cigar to the left side of his mouth and climbed down. Easing the tackle – hired from the army sports store – from his hands, I explained that, to keep the line from snarling into a bird's nest, he should control its run-out with his thumb.

Just as I was warming up after the fifth cast he demanded a go. This time he caught the bank behind him and, somehow, tied himself up like a serial heroine trussed up for the railway line. It took us ten minutes to undo the mess. Then he grabbed the rod ungratefully and climbed back up the rock where there was only room for one.

'You are wasting your time up there,' I called, feeling the initiative slipping away. But I had reckoned without Wall Street.

'Listen, Bud,' he said, mouthing his cigar over to the right side, 'this lake is full of fish and you'll never convince me that there isn't at least one sucker among them.'

Some of us who are hooked become what can only be described as fanatical, putting up with all manner of desperate requirements and even dangerous hazards in our determination to bring the elusive quarry to the bank. It may even entail going for a swim, as this story sent to me by the **Earl of Pembroke** shows.

I was fishing the Frome, in Dorset, on a beat leased by Aylmer Tryon. The water was low and the only hope seemed to lie in some rather anaemic prawns. The best chance of finding a salmon was at the Bunny, a small two-arched bridge with a well-know lie above it and others under the arches. I could see that the first lie was empty but, standing on the bridge and facing upstream, I let down a prawn under the left-hand arch. Almost immediately I was into a fish, the liveliest and most determined survivor I had ever encountered.

The salmon took off downstream, taking a lot of line, and my immediate task was to get it back up through the arch. Suddenly the fish appeared, swimming strongly upstream through the other arch. There was no alternative but to hold hard on the line in the hope that the pressure would bring the fish back downstream, which it did. I was back to my original problem, which was quickly compounded when the fish tore off far below me towards another hazard. There was no hope of bringing it upstream again so, somehow, I had to get the rod through the arch. Wedging the rod in the fork of a nearby tree, I moved below the arch and picked the line out with my gaff, and secured it to the gaff handle, which I stuck in the bank. I then dropped the rod into the water and retrieved it as it came through the arch.

All seemed set for a normal fight to a finish but, as I reeled in, I realised that the salmon was lying just above three hatches through which the river rushes in force towards a mill-pool. As soon as I tried to induce the fish upstream it went straight through one of the hatches, over a wide shelf into the mill-race.

My only option was to wade through the hatch in a very strong current on a slippery bottom, which I managed to do, getting soaked to the waist as well as somewhat alarmed. I then encountered a further obstacle in the form of four feet of anti-poacher wire netting over the wide shelf above the pool. As I did not relish body-surfing on the shelf into the mill-pool, I had to part with the rod yet again.

After checking that the fish was still with me, I groped around the turbulent water of the pool with the gaff and eventually found the line. Once again, I tied the line to the gaff, which I secured on the bank. Then I committed the rod to the current, letting it be swept over the shelf and into the pool. I raced down hoping to intercept it but it had disappeared.

I therefore started to pull on the line and, as yards and yards were thrown on the bank, I realised that I should have hitched the line round the reel. With so much line and backing still on the reel I lay on my stomach and worked the gaff around in the pool, hoping to catch the rod. The tip appeared and I grabbed it. Lying round me was a bird's nest of about forty yards of nylon line which I had torn off so hurriedly that it was entangled in brambles and weeds. It would have taken so long to unravel it that I decided to cut it away and tie the two ends, hoping the fish would remain dormant. I did. The fish was lying exhausted close to the bank at the tail of the pool and was soon grassed after a battle lasting a total of fifty minutes. It weighed 13 pounds, was fresh from the sea and, like many stubborn creatures on this earth was female.

Whereas Lord Pembroke got wet deliberately, that wonderful fisherman **Barry Black** went swimming involuntarily. Here, in his own words, is his account of that highly dangerous experience.

The world's best salmon river in my experience is Norway's Alta, which lies well north of the Arctic Circle, running due north through Lapland to the sea. It is a magnificently strong and rapid river and virtually all fishing has to be done from long, narrow boats just wide enough to accommodate the fisherman in the middle and a boatman at each end. The boatman in the bow has a pair of very short oars with which he drops the boat down each pool slowly enough for the fisherman to cover the fishable water with his fly, which is all that is allowed. The stern boatman has a paddle with which he steers the downward path. Movement upstream can be accomplished only by outboard motor.

When I was fishing there in 1973, the sun hardly sank below the horizon and so we fished at 'night', such as it was, rather than by day, because the sun was so strong that the air temperature reached 86°F and the river became quite warm. On 12 July I set out for the top beat with my wife's cousin, the late Duke of Roxburghe, whose family had 'discovered' the river in 1860 and managed to lease the whole of it for several generations. So far we had each managed to average three fish a day up to 38 pounds, though no monsters had been caught, fifty-pounders not being uncommon.

We were being motored upstream and to save time I changed my fly with my rod resting on my shoulder and the butt in the bottom of the boat. I saw the duke's boat ahead throwing up so much spray as it forged through the rapids that I thought it would make a dramatic photograph. I reached for my camera but, at the same time, the boat lurched heavily to the right and I was ejected into the river.

Though the turbulence was alarming I was not too worried because I knew the drill – get on your back and let yourself be carried down, gradually paddling yourself to the side. I knew that there was some 300 yards of rapids below me before the river hit a rock face and made a right-angled turn into a whirling maelstrom which gradually opened out into smooth water. I was hoping to make the smooth water.

All seemed to be going according to plan until I found myself being sucked under the water again and again, which I put down to the turbulence. I soon began to be dragged down deeper. What was going on? This yo-yo effect continued and I managed to gulp in enough air each time I surfaced to keep going. I knew that by this time I should be through the rapids and round the corner but I couldn't stay on the top long enough to see. Just as I was getting really worried one of the boatmen, who had finally reached me, grabbed me by the hair and slowly towed me towards the shore. The boatmen told me that they had made several previous attempts but each time I had been pulled down by what they thought was the whirlpool to bob up somewhere else.

The mystery was resolved when I tried to stand up. When I had left the boat the fly had stuck in my jacket and, with the rod jammed in the boat, I had taken the line with me and it had wrapped itself round my body. In effect I was being played like a salmon with 300 yards of line and backing swirling in the water. If the water had been ice-cold, as it usually was, I might not have survived.

I was bleeding profusely from five propeller cuts in my legs and arms which, unknown to me, had been inflicted when I had left the boat. These needed stitches at the local hospital but I had to wait half an hour while the doctor dug out an enormous double-hooked Durham Ranger from the bottom of a Norwegian angler.

I must have passed scores of salmon, some of them monsters, as I was tumbled downstream, and my plight could have given them some satisfaction. I got my revenge, however.

After being patched up, having changed my clothes and enjoyed a stiff drink, I was boated to the top of the beat to find I could still cast well enough to get a fine 33-pounder.

18

At least when **Johnnie Johnson**, Britain's top-scoring wartime fighter pilot, went swimming he did it deliberately.

For the last week the bag had stood at unlucky thirteen and was likely to remain so for the river was low and we had very little fishing time left. On our last evening I packed and stowed away my gear as we planned for an early start the next morning. However, it rained steadily throughout the night and, early the following morning, the Carron, in Wester Ross, was high enough for the fly and I decided to have a last hour on the Upper House pool. Since my chest waders were stuffed with newspapers and put away, I wore an old pair of thigh waders with worn rubber soles.

It was raining very hard as I walked the few hundred yards to the pool, where I started from the north bank with a size 8 Garry, casting about eighteen yards towards a rock on the opposite side where, over the years, I have killed a lot of fish from a taking lie behind the rock.

On the third cast I was into a nice fish which ran downstream for fifteen yards, turned and jumped, showing itself to be a grilse of six or seven pounds. He then ran upstream above me, where I thought I would soon have him under control and our fourteenth fish would be in the bag. However, after a few more minutes he took my line round the rock and sulked on the bottom in what I guessed to be about eight feet of water. I could feel the fish nodding from time to time so I just stood there – the tactics being to drown the fish and then cross the river to retrieve it. After twenty minutes or so there was no movement from the salmon so I stuck my rod in a whin bush, stripped off to pants, vest and waders – it was late July – and attempted to cross the river with wading stick and gaff.

The current was far more powerful than I had thought, the rubber soles slipped, and Johnson, wading stick and gaff were carried downstream. After a thorough dunking I managed to stagger out on the south side, walked up the bank to the offending rock and saw the dead salmon still attached to the nylon. Kneeling on the stones, I pulled the line in and tried to gaff the fish but it was too deep so I decided to get into the river, follow the nylon underwater to the fish and gaff it, number fourteen would be on the bank.

Gloved hand on the nylon, I submerged and tried to get down to the fish, but the powerful current collected me like a piece of flotsam, turned me upside down, over and over, and broke the cast. I kept my mouth closed and lay on my back when possible with my arms and legs outstretched and the good river deposited me on the shingle beach of the Lower House pool.

I made an undignified retreat to the cottage, met my startled family, changed into some warm clothes, had a stiff dram and hurried back to the river, thinking that number fourteen may have been beached too. But I never saw that fish again.

Colonel Jackie Ward, a Wiltshire landowner, describes a similar experience in which determination and excitement got the better of discretion.

The Tay was rising fast when I arrived on the bank opposite the well-known Ash Tree pool on the Kinnaird water, which belonged to my family. For some reason I cannot recall, I was alone, without a gillie. I had a bait rod with an odd-looking lure like a sandeel. At any time the Ash Tree is extremely deep and dangerous with its central whirlpool; on that day it was a raging torrent of coloured water from bank to bank. Conditions looked hopeless. As I walked upstream looking for a backwater where a fish might lie I noticed that some trees which were normally well away from the water were being lapped by the river. I threw into a calmer place and on my third cast was into a big fish which took off downstream into the fast water, stripping me down almost to the end of the backing.

I ran after the fish and then came to the trees, which were now surrounded by water. Stupidly, in retrospect – I was in my fifties – I was so determined to get the fish that I plunged into the river, thinking I could wade round the trees, but found myself completely out of my depth. Somehow I managed to avoid being swept into the central current, where I would almost certainly have drowned, by hanging on to overhanging branches, and eventually I stumbled back up the bank rod still in hand. Clear of the trees, I played the fish in the open water and brought it to the gaff. It weighed 31 pounds, not a monster for the Tay in those days but worth the ducking, I thought, as I carried it back. On reflection I think otherwise.

There is a safety axiom in shooting that all the pheasants ever bred would not atone for one man dead. Surely the same applies to salmon, however big.

———————⊃●⊂———————

Sir Geoffrey Johnson Smith, the politician and former television presenter, gives an account of what seems to be the ultimate in lack of self-protection when there is the possibility of losing a good fish.

Like all anglers, I have had my share of despair, bad luck and unexpected joy and success, but have not been involved in anything so dangerous or so self-sacrificing as the mishap which overtook a friend of mine.

He was fishing for salmon in turbulent water. They were showing but not taking. His frustration mounted as the day wore on. Then, suddenly, a fish came to the fly and took.

Minutes later my friend, standing on a rock, had beached his salmon. The line still being taut, the fly sprang out of the fish's mouth and the salmon slithered

back towards the river. The anxious angler lurched forwards to grab it, slipped and fell into the deep water
swirling round the rock. As a colleague ran to save him
he cried out from the engulfing stream:

'Don't bother about me, save the fish!'

Greater love has no man than that he should lay down
his life for a fish!

———————————————⟶•⟵———————————————

The late Lord Alanbrooke came close. The tale is told
by **Peter Bridgeman**, a Northumbrian farming landowner.

Pibe is a remarkable pool on the Driva river in the Sundal
valley in Norway. Immediately upstream are 200 yards of
rapids with enormous boulders and below are 400 yards
of even more turbulent water. Even in the intervening
stretch the currents and whirlpools make it an exciting
place and it is no place for an amateur oarsman. It would
be impossible to follow a salmon out of this pool in a boat.
Many are hooked there because the fish need a rest after
the first rapids and before negotiating the next.

Lord Alanbrooke, who was a regular guest immediately
after the war, nearly came to grief in Pibe. He had been
playing a strong fish and the time had come to get out of
the boat to land it. The gillie stepped out onto the bank
first but fell and lost his grip on the boat. The roar of the
rapids must have drowned his warning shouts, or Lord
Alanbrooke chose to ignore them in his enthusiasm to
prevent the salmon leaving the pool. Whatever the reason.
the Field-Marshal was drifting towards the rapids unaware
that he was on his own.

Fortunately, Pibe runs close to the road and frequently
cars and even buses stop to watch a salmon being played.
On this occasion a bright and brave young Norwegian,
watching from the road, realised the angler's predicament
and, jumping from boulder to boulder down the steep

bank, he leapt into the river and caught the boat just in time.

Lord Alanbrooke was unaware of the drama until he found his 20-pound salmon being netted by a soaked stranger and the gillie sitting on the bank, higher up, nursing a broken ankle. The stranger was also unaware that the short, unassuming person he had rescued was the recently retired Chief of the Imperial General Staff who had done so much to defeat the Germans and liberate Norway in the process.

Many, of course, may think it well worth while to get wet for a good fish, provided there is no real danger. But even then there may be unseen hazards, as this story from **Vic Foot**, a Test river keeper, records.

One of our rods fishing the tidal section of the Nursling beat of the River Test hooked a salmon which, after a few surges up and down, finally took refuge in the luxuriant weed which grows there and is quite a hazard. Usually such a fish eventually digs itself out if the angler is patient, but this one was well and truly fast and seemed content to stay there all night.

I decided to try the usual trick of crossing the river by a bridge and then hooking the line with my bait. I did this several times but, even with the pressure from a different direction, the fish would not move, though I could tell that it was still on. What to do? Heave and hope for the best, possibly breaking the line? That is what most anglers would have done but this one was more determined.

Although the tide was coming in fast, he stripped off every stitch of clothing and waded into the weedbed. He was up to his chin by the time he had handlined and frightened the fish out of the weeds while I held the rod. As he was about to swim, rather than wade back, with all exposed, I could not resist shouting that I had recently seen a 25-pound pike exactly where he was standing. He came out quicker than he went in but we got the fish.

———◦◦———

The danger faced by **David Sussman**, a South African businessman, was rather more real, or at least he believed it to be.

The Mooi river rises in the foothills of the Drakensberg mountain range of·Natal and runs through green and gentle hill down the Natal Midlands to join the great Tugala river south of Rorke's Drift. In the upper reaches, above 3,000 feet, it is cool from the melting snow of the Berg and rich in food for the wild brown trout for which it is famous. Four miles of this part of the Mooi run through the lovely farm, Drayton, owned by my friends Michael and Gaye Youngelson.

Fishing the Mooi is a privileged experience. The summer days are invariably warm and sunny, whilst the early mornings and evenings can be cold and even frosty. The hills and meadows provide food and cover for a great variety of fauna and flora. Jackal buzzards and black eagles glide high above and the harsh cry of the ha-di-ha, the black ibis, rings out through the valleys. Walking the banks of the river the angler often puts up a grey reebok or a grysbock and the sand patches are covered with their spoor, as well as that of caracal cats, otters, snakes and many species of birds.

Parts of the river require wading, since the banks of the deeper pools are often overhung by wattle and Cape willow. We tend to wear shorts and plimsolls for this purpose because of the warmth of the summer days.

It was late afternoon on such a day as I stood waist-deep in the tail of a promising pool, trying to place my Walker's

Killer upstream under an overhanging branch. Two or three lost flies later my side cast succeeded. The fly had not yet sunk when there was an explosion and I was hooked into one of the biggest trout I had seen in the Mooi. Keeping as tight a line on the furious fish as I dared, I edged crab-wise across the slippery rocks on the riverbed towards the bank, where I planned to climb out through the bushes and lead the fish downstream to a clear patch where I could net it.

Having reached the bank, I stretched out for a thickish branch behind me and kicked into the muddy wall to pull myself clear and scramble up. The branch was flexible and moved in my hand. I glanced over my shoulder and saw that I was firmly grasping a two-inch-thick, five-foot-long, bright green and very angry snake. Green mamba! One of the world's deadliest reptiles.

I flung the snake away from me as hard as I could, praying that it would not turn on me. With the impetus I spun round and fell with a great splash into the river. Still holding my rod high, I surfaced to find that the snake had bounced off a branch and dropped into the water about a foot away from my face. There were now three hyperactive creatures within a few feet of each other, each with his own urgent agenda: the trout, terrified by the turmoil about it; myself, tail-walking like a marlin back to the bank; and the snake, which thrashed its way – thank heavens – to the opposite bank.

I shot up my bank and through the bushes as though they did not exist and stood panting from terror and exertion, trying to collect both my composure and line, which was wrapped round innumerable branches. With difficulty I finally fenced the line out of the bushes and wound it onto the reel. The trout was still hooked and I was able to net it where I had originally planned. In gratitude for my narrow escape I held it gently in the current until it recovered to swim safely away, no doubt as shaken as I was. I estimated it to weigh just on 2 pounds, a grand fish for that river.

When I returned to the farmhouse to recount my breathless tale my friend Michael, with what I thought to be rather exaggerated patience, explained that, in Natal, the green mamba was to be found only in the coastal plain area and that what I had encountered was a common and harmless grass snake. He also showed some scepticism about the trout's weight.

He may have been right but the experience is not my favourite of many days spent on the Mooi before and since.

Snakes are my own worst phobia and I have been gratified to find that others share this horror. One such is **Gary Brooker**, the singer and composer of popular songs.

Some time in 1981 I was in Oregon with American friends in pursuit of steelhead trout – magnificent fish which run up to twenty or even thirty pounds in some states. My aim was to catch one over ten pounds and after fishing some mountain rivers in the Portland area we moved to the beautiful Deschutes river in the high desert area.

To reach the various fishing stretches my friend and guide, Bob Tollman, had a very fast jet-boat which could negotiate water only six inches deep. The drive, at what seemed to be about sixty miles an hour, was an experience in itself. I would be dropped on the bank to walk as far upstream as I liked and then fish the water down with a fly, yard by yard.

While walking upstream on the first day I was confronted by a bull snake about five feet long and as thick as your arm, sitting on the path. When I told Bob about it later he said, 'Oh, bull snakes are harmless. It's the rattlers you need to watch out for.'

If there is one thing I hate it is a snake and the thought

that I might encounter a rattler was terrifying.

The following day Bob dropped me off at Blackberry Hole and I began my walk up the river. The bank was covered with low sage-brush and I made my way through it very carefully, stamping the ground every few yards. Then, after watching carefully for anything slithering, I would gingerly go forward a few more paces. I had heard the rattle of the rattlesnake in TV films and suddenly I heard the same sound in real life – a rapid click-click-click-click and very close.

There was only one thing for it. I ran for all I was worth, but the sound pursued me and the snake seemed to be right behind me, clicking its rattle louder and louder and longer and longer. After running some seventy-five yards I stopped for breath, hoping that I was clear. The rattle had stopped and I saw why.

Behind me, draped over the sage bushes, was fifty yards of fly line and backing. My heavy reel, needed to accommodate so much line, had a rather loud check.

I did eventually manage to catch a 12-pound steelhead which I have, mounted, at home. When I reached the house where I was staying the people were out so I bought a few cans of beer at the supermarket and sat down in the sunshine. After the third can, a tune and some words to go with it came into my head and resulted in a song to commemorate my days on the Deschutes – 'The Angler'.

Robert Lamphere, an officer of the American FBI and author of the recently published *The FBI/KGB War*, had a more fruitful encounter.

As a boy growing up in the 1930s, it was not often that I returned home with no fish after a day spent working the Saint Regis River in the Bitteroot Range of Western

Montana. But on one warm August day – actually hot for the mountain country – it looked as though I would. The water was very low and the trout were taking nothing that I could offer. It was also very easy to spook them, however carefully one approached the water.

Still hoping, however, as all born fishermen do, I crept up Indian-style on one of the deeper holes with extreme care, confident that the fish would not see me. To my great disappointment, after so much effort, I saw that there was already pandemonium in the pool. It was not my shadow but a big black snake which was causing the trout to scurry around in such alarm. I could see that it already had a 9-inch trout in its mouth.

Fortunately, the snake and I reached the bank at about the same moment and, after some argument about ownership which I won, I went home with one small but fat trout, which saved a blank day. All God's creatures have their uses.

<hr />

To return to episodes involving immersion in the fishes' environment, often with nothing on the hook, a story from **The Earl of Kimberley** seems worthy of record.

I had invited Max Hastings, the *Daily Telegraph* editor and author, to fish with me on the Castle Grant beat of the Spey. He duly arrived and the first thing I did, as I do with all my guests there, was to warn him of the dangers of the very deep pools. I specifically told him that, though he is a big and powerful man, he would be most unwise to try to fish down the pools without the help of a wading stick, not just for extra support against the current when moving but to probe the depth as he advanced.

Admittedly, a wading stick is a nuisance when you are casting and for that reason, or because of the courageous spirit he had shown in his journalistic coverage of the

Falklands War, Max ignored my advice. He waded boldly out into the river, only to disappear completely in short order. Happily he reappeared a few yards downstream, wet through, cold, but definitely wiser.

As three other fishermen had done the same disappearing trick, I decided to constitute my own sub-aqua club and appointed Max Hastings as chairman.

Those who had the pleasure of knowing the late **Lady Sopwith** will recall that she was a formidable woman as well as being a good clean shot and an insatiable angler. To see her on the river bank in her green outfit, with a diamond salmon brooch in her hat, was to realise right away that here was an angler of determination. There are many stories about her and two in particular are typical of the spirit she displayed when, in her late seventies, she insisted that her heart-pacemaker should be inserted on her left side so that she could get her gun up!

On her first visit to the Delfur beat of the Spey in early April, her ladyship was put in the care of a good but irascible gillie who did not take kindly to a woman who, he believed, was probably a beginner. He settled her in an anchored boat at the top of the long Two Stones pool and suggested that she should begin to spin it down while he lowered the boat down on a rope.

'How far would you like me to cast?' she asked, in all innocence.

'Och, as far as ye can,' the gillie replied curtly, believing that five yards was probably the maximum.

With a mighty whoosh Lady Sopwith landed the bait high in a bush on the other side of the river. 'Now I'll step out of the boat while you row over and get it,' she said sweetly.

The two became good friends and on another occasion, some seasons later, the same gillie was boating her ladyship down another pool of the Delfur beat. A fish showed a long way below and the gillie, now well aware of her casting prowess, suggested she should try to cover it immediately. Whoosh! With a mighty cast the bait zoomed downstream but, regrettably, so did Lady Sopwith, who went head first into the water.

It was doubtful whether the gillie could swim but, thankfully, Lady Sopwith could and after being totally submerged and touching the bottom she managed to get ashore, holding to the boat, her hat with the diamond brooch still firmly on her head.

It was quite an achievement for an overweight lady in her late sixties. The rod was recovered and not even dignity was lost because she waded ashore highly amused by the experience. She insisted that, from then on, the site of her involuntary swim should be called Mum's Pool, and so it was known to all who had the privilege to fish there with her and Sir Thomas.

It would be a poor gillie who deposited his charge in the water but less professional boatmen may do so, as **Richie Benaud**, the former Australian cricket captain, records.

On 15 October 1981, a day I shall always remember, my wife, Daphne, and I arrived at a Sydney wharf for a day's fishing with business clients and friends. The owner and captain of the cabin cruiser which we were to board had spent the early morning carefully studying the tides, checking the force of the wind and charting the course for the voyage.

He then informed us that to reach the cabin cruiser all four people – with their fishing tackle, bags and all the

31

food and drink – would embark into a small row-boat equipped with an outboard motor. At that stage the row-boat was on dry land some fifteen feet from the water's edge. Having recently suffered a neck injury, for which I was wearing a neck-brace, I was unable to assist the captain and my wife in pushing the boat into the water, an activity which produced so much four-letter language from the captain that I was helpless on the ground with laughter anyway.

My attitude was not improved when it took the captain twenty minutes to start the outboard motor while we loaded the vessel. Finally, on the nautical instruction 'For God's sake take that rope off that thing on the wharf', I boarded, rope in hand, and the captain, exuding an air of quiet confidence, announced that the day's adventure was about to begin.

Sadly, instead of turning left, as he should, the captain and helmsman turned right, towards the wharf, which was about a yard away. The whole boat overturned, depositing all its contents, human and inanimate, into the drink. In keeping with tradition, the captain was the last to leave.

When I surfaced I could hear the gallant captain assuring my wife that he would come and save her and I would have liked to commend her for the Wife of the Year Award as she responded, 'Don't worry about me, you pillock! Save Richie. . . . He can't swim.' Though weighed down by an expensive Gucci outfit, I managed to make it to shallower water, about four feet deep, assisted by my neck-brace, which seemed to act like water-wings. Our band regrouped there and guided the row-boat to a mooring. We did manage to salvage some things but, of the Benauds' property, various expensive reels and a Swiss knife with twenty-six attachments (including a fish-scaler not used on the day in question) remained on the bottom and could not be recovered.

At the end of the adventure the captain suggested that the trip should be resumed on the following day but the

Benauds decided that, before this invitation could be accepted, we should seek the permission of our insurance company.

Of all the anglers who have been dunked, surely none did it with greater grace than a certain Scottish lady, as described by His Grace **the Duke of Fife.**

According to a Deeside gillie of my acquaintance, Her Majesty Queen Elizabeth the Queen Mother, who used to be a keen salmon angler, was fishing a certain pool on the Dee at Ballater where the opposite side was under different ownership. As the pool was wide enough for two to fish from opposite banks without mutual interference, another lady, wearing chest waders, eased her way into the river, guiding herself by her long wading stick.

When as deeply in as she dared to go, which was to her waist, the lady suddenly recognised the royal angler on the other side. As their eyes met, and almost as a reflex action, the lady dipped low in curtsy, filling her waders with Dee water in the process. Under she went, having to be rescued by two gillies who were, fortunately, close by.

The Queen Mother's response to this aquatic respect is not recorded.

The story has often been told with variations. Mine is the correct version, and I even know the name of the unfortunate lady angler, which, since she is deceased, will remain a secret with me.

Rivers, which are always laws unto themselves, are no respecters of royalty, or of anyone else, and the **Queen Mother** has not escaped a wetting.

Two Deeside gillies met in Banchory while shopping for fishing tackle. Said the short one to the much taller, 'You had the Queen Mother fishing your beat yesterday!'

'Ay,' the tall one replied.

'Did ye have a good day?'

'No, it was a catastrophe,'

'Oh Lord! Did Her Majesty lose a big fush?' the short one asked.

'No. It was worse than that,' said the tall one. 'I told her to cast for a fush from where I was standing. The water was up to my knees but when she moved it came up to her navel. I hadn't noticed she was wearing only thigh waders.'

Gillies are, understandably, reticent about retailing stories concerning their royal charges but the reactions of three of them have come my way.

For the first I am grateful to **Mrs William Govett**, wife of the merchant banker, who owns the lovely beat of Upper Blackhall on the Dee.

Alec, a gillie who worked for the Govetts, was assisting the Queen Mother when a fisherman on the other side slipped and was in difficulties. By the time Alec managed to get a rope to the man, by dint of great effort and no little danger to himself, the angler was half drowned and within inches of deep, strong water which would have finished him. Using all his strength Alec managed to haul him out.

The fisherman, unaware of the royal guest who was watching, recovered enough to put his hand in his pocket, produced a soaked wallet full of notes and gave the ghillie £1 before staggering off to change.

Alec's only comment to the Queen Mother was: 'He didn't value his life very highly, did he?'

Viscount Thurso recalls another incident involving the Queen Mother.

This is a true story of the unusual prowess of the late David Sinclair, who for many years was River Superintendent on the Thurso river in Caithness, and who, as a gillie in our younger years, taught me to fish. David was gillieing for Queen Elizabeth the Queen Mother one day when she was fortunate to hook a salmon in the Castle Pool on my beat of the Thurso. Her Majesty played the fish with skill until at last she brought it in to the bank below her feet.

At that point the bank is grassy and steeply sloping so David clambered down to gaff the fish. As he threw it up the bank above him, intending to follow it and dispatch it with his priest, the fly fell out of the salmon's mouth. The fish then gave a flick of its tail and shot into the air over David's shoulder, heading back for the river. Instinctively, David stuck out his gaff and caught the fish in mid-air.

This time he made no mistake and climbed up the bank holding firmly on to the salmon while the Queen Mother remarked, 'David, if I had not seen that with my own eyes I would never have believed it.'

The relaxed relationship between the royal family and those who serve them in Scotland is quite remarkable and is exemplified by this simple story told to me by the fisherman concerned.

One of the postmen who used to deliver letters in the Balmoral area was passing the time of day with a fisherman and remarked that he had seen and spoken with the Queen that morning. The observant angler than remarked, 'Do you think Her Majesty saw that big hole in the seat of your trousers?'

'Nae, nae, she couldna,' the postman replied with confidence.

'What makes you so sure?'

'I remembered it was there so I just kept my arse to the hill.'

Every year there is an estate party at Balmoral which the royal family seem to enjoy as much as the staff. On one occasion the Balmoral gillie, Donald Forbes, was dancing with the Queen when her Majesty stopped in the middle of the floor and presented Donald to her mother.

The Queen Mother smiled and said, 'I'm very glad to see you, Donald, because there are several fishing questions I want to ask you.'

She then exchanged partners with the Queen and Donald and the Queen Mother danced off together, chattering away.

I am told that Donald believes that he may be the only gillie to have tripped the light fantastic with two queens during one dance, though he is disinclined to talk about it.

The other royal servants are equally tight-lipped, but, occasionally, a story does reach the river-side grapevine.

The present Prince of Wales was fly fishing on the Tay and the day had been blank for him but, as sometimes happens, he hooked a salmon on what was intended to be his last cast. The fish was obviously sizeable, and fresh, and took rather a long time to play and beach.

By the time His Royal Highness had returned to Balmoral, over the hills in the Dee valley, he found that he was late for dinner. The curtains were drawn in the dining room, which implied that the family had started the evening meal without him.

To announce his arrival – and to account for its lateness – the Prince found an open window and noiselessly pushed in his 19-pound salmon, head first, through the curtains. All the royal family and their guests could see were the cold eyes of a large dead fish. But they got the message.

———————⟶○⟵———————

While the Prince of Wales gave up shooting for a while, his interest in fishing has never diminished and began at a very early age, as witness this charming story told to me by **Bernard Aldrich**, the head river keeper at Broadlands, as we sat in the fishing hut there.

When he was ten years old, Prince Charles and his sister, Princess Anne, were staying with Lord Mountbatten at Broadlands. Uncle Dickie, as they called him, decided to give them some excitement by enlisting their help in catching a salmon.

A fish of about twelve pounds was found to be lying in a good taking place under a rickety old cattle bridge, close to the centre supports. Bernard realised that provided Lord Mountbatten, who was not really a keen fisherman, was given a running commentary on where to place his bait the fish could probably be caught.

As Bernard explained to his illustrious master, who was then the nation's defence supremo, the drill was to stand some distance above the bridge and drop a prawn slowly downstream, to instructions given from someone who was watching the fish through cracks in the floor of the bridge. Once the fish took the prawn it was bound to rush downstream and the only way to land it was to slacken the line so that the spotter on the bridge could hook it with a gaff, while the fisherman put a couple of half hitches round the reel handle and dropped the rod into the river. The spotter, who was usually Bernard, then

37

pulled the rod through the bridge and the fisherman, who had meanwhile run down the bank, could then play it in the normal way.

On this occasion the two royal children were down on their knees serving as spotters, as well as Bernard.

To excited cries, the prawn slowly appeared in front of the fish, which took it first time. Unfortunately, Uncle Dickie did not slacken the line to let the fish run and as it thrashed about on the surface it disengaged the hook, to the intense disappointment of all present.

Prince Charles's response was 'My Daddy wouldn't have lost the fish!'

No doubt, since then, Prince Charles has lost his own quota of hooked salmon.

With so few kings left in the world only one kingly story has come my way – from **Nicole Law**, the French wife of Frank Law, the businessman.

His Majesty the King of Morocco announced, 'We are going fishing.'

'Me too?' I asked, knowing that women were rarely included on such occasions.

'Yes, you too. And do not try to be difficult. I will give you some helpers.'

And so we went to a beautiful lake in the mountains where, weight for weight, there was the same amount of trout as water. His Majesty was on one side of the lake and I was facing him on the other, flanked by two conscript soldiers who looked as bewildered as I was. They set up the spinning rod, handed it to me and stood back.

With the first throw I hooked one of the soldiers by his battle fatigues, so securely that it took several minutes for his comrade to free him. Meanwhile His Majesty was reeling in one trout after another. After further attempts in which I hooked the other soldier and all the nearby bushes the hook finally landed in the water about three feet away from me. As I stood watching it His Majesty shouted, 'Reel it in! Reel it in!'

'No,' I replied. 'It was far too difficult to get it out there.'

At that moment a trout took the bait, static as it was, and I jerked up the rod and there was the fish, dancing in the air.

'Drop it back, drop it back!' the king shouted.

I did so and to everyone's amazement landed the trout.

Unprepared to push my luck further, I spent the rest of the afternoon watching the others. When each angler lined up his catch at the end of the day His Majesty asked for mine. I told him, 'One trout, three bushes and two soldiers.'

I still don't understand why he never asked me to go fishing again.

I do not know if maharajas count as kings, but the following story, contributed by **Mary Carswell,** the manageress of the Banchory Lodge Hotel, deserves in any case to be placed on record.

A former Maharaja of Jaipur, who had never fished for salmon before, was taken as a guest on a Scottish river and placed in the professional hands of Findlay McIntosh, one of the best-known gillies. To avoid the bankside trees he was boated out into a pool and, being a fast learner, was soon into a good fish.

Under McIntosh's guidance His Royal Highness, as the gillie had been told to address him, played the fish and had it coming towards the boat. As the gillie lowered the net into the water the Maharaja lowered the tip of his rod and the fly came out of the salmon's mouth.

It was too much for McIntosh, who roared, 'Ye blithering idiot! What did ye dae that for?' Quickly realising his error, he apologised profusely but feared he must have alienated the Maharaja for good. The Maharaja was too polite, however, to show any anger.

They continued to fish and, as happens, especially in boats, they discussed their respective families. Findlay, who was a widower, had an only daughter and spoke of her with pride. The morning passed without another fish and when the gillie bade goodbye to the Maharaja, who had to leave then, he bowed low in mute expression of further apology for his gaffe.

About a month later a letter arrived for the gillie at his cottage. It was an invitation from the Maharaja for Findlay and his daughter to spend two weeks at one of his palaces in Rajasthan, all his travelling expenses being paid. This they did with enormous enjoyment, even being met on their arrival with a pipe band!

Findlay was never able to decide whether he would have been asked if he had not lost his temper. Perhaps the Maharaja had never been bawled out before in his life and admired his courage:

I do not know if the Queen Mother was in the habit of taking her corgis with her when she went salmon fishing, but dogs are common riverside companions and learn to take an interest. My husband's old springer spaniel, Scoop, loved trout fishing so much that she would tuck herself into the bankside vegetation at the point where she thought her master would be likely to rise and hook a fish, and become wildly excited when this happened, watching intently when the trout came to the net. She never caused a disaster but there have been others that did, as the late **Ken Robinson**, a magnificent fisherman, describes.

A guest fishing the Fawn stream on the Inchmarlo beat of the Dee, in the spring, foul-hooked a large salmon with a bait and had a tremendous tussle with it in the rather high water. He did his best to keep it in the pool, but from the knock-knock way it was playing I could see that it would eventually take off downstream and, after about half an hour, off it went into the next pool, where the current was much faster, with the guest struggling along the bank to keep up with it, followed by me with the net and his gun dog, a large springer spaniel called Duke.

The same performance took place, with the fish running through into the next pool, called the Laird's Cast. I told the guest, who was now getting rather tired, that if he did not kill it there he would have a terrible job following it down the next, very rapid, pool, the Lower Seaties, because thick bushes and trees lined the bank and he would have to go down in the water, which was deep in places. When the fish finally decided to go down farther still towards Aberdeen, he suggested that I should take the rod, but, being considerably older and disinclined to go swimming, I convinced him that he should have the honour. So off the angler went, followed by the faithful Duke.

I, and another rod who had become interested in the performance, waited at the House Pool for the intrepid fisherman to appear round the corner, which blinded our vision as he struggled with the monster in the very rough water. He duly appeared, with the fish still on. He was wet through and so exhausted by stumbling about over the Dee's boulder-strewn bottom that he insisted that I should take the rod from him. This time I could not refuse and once again off went the fish through more rapids into the lowest pool on our beat, the famous Roe Pot.

For ease of fishing, the Roe Pot is equipped with a number of piers, which are the envy of the opposite side, and we hoped to net the fish off the first one, where the water was less turbulent. The fish was still keen on reaching Aberdeen, however, and, gradually, we went down one pier after another, each time bringing the fish near but not quite into the net. We could see why

it had fought for more than two hours – it was a fresh-run springer in the big twenties, hooked in the back fin.

When we got on to the last pier, the guest, who was handling the net, called to me, 'You'll have to bring it in now Ken, if we are going to get it.' Sadly 'Get it' were the words of command on which Duke, the spaniel, had been trained to retrieve a pheasant. Already overexcited by the battle, he leapt on the salmon just as I was drawing it to the net and the great fish flapped away free.

It was a case of one springer saving the life of another.

The case of a bankside dog which performed a more positive service is recounted by **John Fowles**, chairman of Gowrings Garages and Leisure Group.

A young man on leave from the army, and in need of a break, was advised by his father to approach a crusty old relative who owned some fishing in Scotland, though it had always proved extremely difficult to persuade him to allow any member of the family to enjoy it. To everyone's surprise the old man grudgingly agreed to allow the young soldier half a day's fishing.

He had been fishing for only a short time when a back cast with his salmon fly rod engaged something behind and, to loud yelps and whines, he found that his hook was firmly embedded in the posterior of a large yellow labrador, which took off across the field, stripping line off with every bound. The young man could do nothing but hang on to his rod until, when all the backing had been run out, the cast snapped.

The dog had created so much distressing noise that it had aroused the owner of the fishing, who was seen by the angler bearing down, shaking and red in the face. Being convinced that this was the last time he or any branch of his family would be allowed to fish, he was surprised to find his old relative in rare good humour. Laughing gleefully, the old man slapped the soldier on the shoulder and cried: 'Well done! That dog belongs to a neighbour and is nothing but a damn nuisance. I've been trying to dissuade it from coming here for years and now I think you've probably done it. You are welcome to come here and fish whenever you like.'

Dogs sitting on river banks must have been hooked hundreds of times, but not as often as anglers have hooked other people – and themselves. Such accidents have often had tragic consequences and nobody should fling a fly or bait about, or be in the vicinity, without wearing protective glasses. Happily, there have been many occasions when the accident, though painful, has generated more amusement than injury, as the late **Ken Robinson** recalls.

After dinner on a hot summer day, two keen and elderly fishermen returned to the Inchmarlo beat of the River Dee to fish the darkening. When the light was very dim one of them hooked a good salmon and the other stopped fishing to gillie for him.

After a good fight, the lucky angler retreated a few yards up the bank, with his rod well bent, so that his friend would have plenty of room at the water's edge to net the fish. The friend was about to accomplish this when, perhaps as a result of excessive pressure from the angler, the fly sprang out of the fish's mouth and impaled itself deeply in the netsman's thumb.

It was too dark for the angler, above, to see what had happened. All he knew was that there was something on the hook agitatedly pulling hard – which, understandably, he assumed to be the fish.

'Have you got it yet?' the angler shouted above the

noise of the stream.

'It's gone. For God's sake slacken the line' was the agonised response.

'What do you mean, it's gone? I can feel it playing. It's still on. Stop shouting and net the bloody thing.'

The rod pressure increased and the thumb was jerked ever more painfully, for the angler's hearing was not all that good. It was some time before the injured netsman was able to grab the cast in the gloom and convince his friend that he had been playing his thumb on an increasingly short and taut line.

───────────◦───────────

The palm for an hilarious account of such an accidental hooking must, however, go to **Roger de Vere** for the following story, which he knows to be true.

In the far north of Canada two anglers set out with a guide to fish a lake from a canoe. As was customary when big fish were the quarry, they used very large wooden plug baits, each carrying several fearsomely large treble hooks. The fishermen were sitting back to back while the guide paddled the canoe.

One of them decided to change his plug and put the one he had taken off on the seat. Having put on his new plug, he sat down heavily on the old one and jumped up with a scream as one of the very sharp hooks pierced deep into his behind. Startled by the cry of pain, his companion jumped up too and, somehow, became impaled on another of the trebles in the same region. Here, then, were two large men in the middle of a lake joined together by the buttocks like Siamese twins and in considerable pain whenever they twisted or turned in an effort to get the hooks out.

The guide rowed them to shore, and they clambered out as best they could. The guide then inserted his hand between their backsides to see if he could free at least one of them. While doing so one of them winced and the reaction impaled the guide's thumb on yet another of the hooks. Two were back to back and the third had his hand held by the bait between their bottoms. How the fish must have laughed!

Somehow they walked a longish distance to a small hospital serviced by a young Canadian lady doctor. Having cut a way through their trousers to expose the situation, the doctor, realising the uniqueness of the case, insisted on taking a photograph 'for her medical records' before attempting to separate them surgically. Understandably, the patients all objected, loudly, but she was adamant and had the whip hand. I saw the photograph and was told the extraordinary tale by the doctor herself.

Michael Clark, the former deputy chairman of Plessey, has sent me an account of an accidental hooking which was unfunny at the time but is amusing in retrospect, particularly in the laconic way it is recorded in his fishing book.

There was a certain famous lieutenant-general who came to fish with us on the second day of his honeymoon, observing that he would not miss a good day on the Test merely because of having just married. He hooked his new bride in the thumb and had to driver her to Southampton General Hospital for a minor operation. His entry in the fishing book reads:

Fish	Flavia
Weight	112 lb
Total	1
Fly	Nuptial Delight
Conditions	Stormy

Most of us will remember **Ginger Rogers** as the brilliant dancing partner of Fred Astaire and as a talented actress. She also became hooked on angling at an early age and, in spite of her natural agility, managed to become hooked literally, as she described in a letter to me.

One day during the 1940s my then husband, Jack Briggs, and his long-time friend, Jackie Cooper, were in the mood to go fishing. So I chimed in that, since it was salmon-fishing time, I'd love to join them to go down the Rogue river in our flat-bottomed fishing boat. This type of boat takes the flow of the river with very little need for the use of oars, except to push off a rock in the stream.

I placed a lure at the end of my 20 lb breaking strain line and off we went – the three of us casting from one boat. I had decided to take my waders so that I could eventually leave the boat and reduce the chance of getting caught in their backlash. After an hour I asked Jack to row the boat to the bank, where I wanted to put my waders on. The two Jacks continued to cast from the boat while I began to cast my line from the bank.

After about twenty casts I hooked and landed a steelhead of 6 3/4 pounds – the only fish caught thus far. After putting the fish in my bag I started to cast again and let out a loud Indian whoop as my rod bent double! My husband rowed ashore at speed, convinced that, with all that excitement, I must be into a big steelhead. It was bigger than he thought. All I could do was to point to my backside and ask him to free my lure from my wader breeches.

———————◗◖———————

Ginger's predicament was not deserved, but the **Earl of Dalhousie** recalls a case that was.

Billy Flynn, a gillie of great renown in the Caresville area of Ireland, was looking after a guest who was fishing with a lure called a Demon. This had three double hooks in tandem linked together by gut, and is not seen around much these days. The day was Sunday, when salmon fishing is allowed in Ireland, unlike Scotland, where it is prohibited.

Billy was out of sight in the fishing hut, having his lunch, when the rod was fortunate enough to land a salmon. While he was extricating the hooks from the fish's mouth the salmon gave a strong flap and hooked both of the angler's hands firmly together in an attitude of prayer.

His shouts for help brought Billy to the scene and he was able to kill the fish and cut the gut. He then drove the angler to the doctor for the appropriate treatment. As the patient entered the surgery he looked, for all the world, as though he were praying for forgiveness for some dreadful sin.

Referring to the incident later, Billy declared that through the medium of the fish the good Lord had made the angler pay an appropriate penance – for being a Protestant and fishing on Sunday!

———————◦———————

Many anglers have experienced occasions when the annoyance of being caught on the bottom of the river has led to the capture of a fish. A salmon either takes or is foul-hooked as fly or bait is pulled free. In this true story the reward was delayed for an hour or so.

Ian Anderson, the gillie on Upper Blackhall on the Dee, was assisting a fisherman whose fly had caught on an underwater obstruction. He pulled hard on the line by hand and the fly flew back, embedding itself under Anderson's left eye. He drove to the surgery in Banchory with the large Tosh fly hanging down under his glasses. Two old ladies in the waiting room could not take their eyes off him.

The Banchory doctors deal with scores of such accidents in a season and their normal practice is to cut the shank of the hook and bring the remainder out by pushing it through the locally anaesthetised skin. This time the doctor was so taken with the fly that he said he would avoid cutting it so that it could be used again. Anderson demurred but the doctor was adamant that the fly should be saved. He injected a local anaesthetic, made an incision and removed the fly.

Feeling that fate was somehow taking a hand, Anderson tied the fly back on when he reached the river and, with the first cast, his fortunate fisherman hooked a 14-pound salmon.

Incidentally, **Ian Anderson** is the only gillie I have seen who carries an umbrella, a collapsible one which he takes out of his pocket as soon as it begins to rain or snow. He also carries a shooting-stick. Both are out of character for Scottish gillies, some of whom eschew even a waterproof, whatever the weather. But why get wet or unnecessarily weary during the hours – usually all too long these days – when the rod is flogging away without result?

In any case, Ian is something of an oddity on a salmon river. He was a *Daily Mail* photographer but gave it up for a quieter life by the river. He has no regrets, in spite of what must be one of the worst experiences to befall any gillie anywhere in the world. . .

On 23 May 1979 a young Deeside gillie was walking back from the Middle Blackhall beat carrying a new 17 ½-foot carbon-fibre fly rod over his shoulder. As he reached the fishing hut the rod tip touched the overhead electricity cable, which carried 11,000 volts. The owner had arranged with the electricity company to have the wires raised to a safer level just a few days later. When the gillie failed to return home by midnight his wife went in search and found him dead on the path. She telephoned Ian Anderson, the gillie on the next beat up the river, for assistance.

When Anderson arrived he confirmed that his friend was dead and assumed that he must have had a heart attack. He picked up the rod, and as he too touched the wires there was a blue flash and he was thrown some twenty feet down the road. Miraculously, he survived. He felt as though his whole body was on fire, his hand was burned, and there was a hole in one of his gumboots. Without the gumboots he would almost certainly have been electrocuted.

The following morning he discovered a hole in his foot where the massive electric discharge had escaped to earth. He was taken into hospital, where the physician remarked that he had seen such 'exit holes' on the bodies of several electrocution fatalities but never on anyone who had survived.

Later Anderson received a present from his grand-daughter – a tee-shirt bearing a large clenched fist grasping an electric flash and the words 'Grand-dad – Tested to 11,000 volts'.

I have never been subjected to a severe electric shock but I have experienced a hair-raising twenty minutes fearing that I was about to be struck by lightning. This happened while I was fishing from a boat on the Junction Pool on the Kinnaird beat of the Tay. The boatman was John Lorimer, one of my favourite gillies, a quiet man of great charm and good sense.

The fish had been dour and we were going to pack up when I had fished the long pool down with a wooden Devon, especially as the skies were darkening fast and a storm was obviously brewing. Within a few minutes, thunder was rolling and lightning was flashing as the storm grew closer. We saw my husband, who was fly-fishing the pool below with a long carbon-fibre rod, hurriedly walking away from the river to our vehicle.

The rain had begun to fall, the intervals between the thunder and lightning flashes were down to a few seconds and gusts of wind were making fishing difficult. We were so near the end of the pool that I decided on just a few more casts. Suddenly there was a flash of lightning which hit the overhead cables close by, extinguishing the lights in the cottage in front of us and, as it turned out, in the big house. I was terrified but did not like to show it. I looked at Lorimer. 'We'd best be going, madam,' he said. 'Fish never take in a thunderstorm, anyway.'

At that very moment there was a bang on my line. 'I have news for you, John,' I cried. 'I'm into a fish.'

With delight on his face, he rowed me to the shingle where we could beach the salmon. With the rain in torrents and the lightning flashing all round us I climbed out of the boat to do battle with the fish, which was big and way out in the rough water.

The peak of my cap suddenly gave way and water streamed into my cleavage as I had failed to zip up my coat. I heard Lorimer behind me asking if he could help as I tried to pull up the zip. Suddenly I became aware of the shining metal of the reel and, remembering the story that it could attract lightning, tried to cover it with my hand.

I was thoroughly frightened but determined to get the fish – which, eventually, I did. It was a 19-pound sea-licer and the only fish caught by any of the guests that day.

As we rowed across to the car with my rod safely down and the storm abating, I asked Lorimer, 'Could I have been struck?'

'No, not with a glass-fibre rod,' he replied.

'What would you have done if I had been fishing with a carbon rod? I asked.

'Cut the line, put the rod down and got as far away it as possible.'

My husband, who was in the car listening to the five o'clock news, had assumed that we had been sheltering from the storm. He admonished me for fishing on and assured me that any wet rod is dangerous in a thunderstorm.

'What would you have done if you had hooked that fish?' I asked him as Lorimer appeared, carrying my splendid catch.

He thought for only a moment. 'The same as you did.'

As fishermen soon discover, gillies are a race apart. Some can even take being hooked by a guest with good grace, as Ian Anderson did, and most of them are especially tactful when their employers are involved, as **Major Derek Foster**, owner of the famed Park beat on the Dee remembers.

Some years ago my gillie, George Cooper, was teaching my wife to fish from a boat on our beat of the Aberdeenshire Dee, which is called Park. She made a bad cast and hooked him firmly in his waders. Horrified apologies poured from her but Cooper had no problem in soothing her anxiety.

'Don't worry,' he said, as he extracted the hook and inspected the damage. 'We'll take advantage of it. We'll change the flee — seeing that it is in the boat!'

Bob Findlay, the gillie on Tilbouries beat of the Aberdeenshire Dee, used his gaff to great effect.

I was fishing the end of the long Weir Pool on the Grandhome beat of the Don in Aberdeenshire when I saw a well-known Brigadier making his way along the edge of the weir to spin the top of the pool. Before doing so he had tied his large labrador to a tree, using binder twine. I watched him move gingerly down the face of the weir, with the water about calf-height, to a small concrete block just big enough to stand on.

He had just begun to cast when his dog, which always accompanied him, chewed his way through the twine and set off after him along the top of the weir. I shouted to the Brigadier but he could not hear me above the noise of the rushing water.

Momentarily, the dog tried to remain a few yards behind his master, as he usually did, but unable to withstand the weight of the water he leaped forward knocking the Brigadier into the turbulent pool. The dog had no problem in swimming out but for his master, in chest waders, it was not so easy. Fortunately, he managed to remain afloat and as he reached the tail of the pool I managed to get my gaff into his wader straps and haul him ashore – undignified but, at least, not drowned.

The Brigadier's reaction was interesting. He took it out on the dog.

As salmon fishers spend so much time in the close company of gillies, tact is needed on their part if they are to get the unstinted service which can make so much difference to the enjoyment and the catch. The **Rt Hon. David Steel, MP**, tells a story which demonstrates the point.

There is a fine painting at Makerstoun of a famous gillie, Rob of the Trews, born in 1779, of whom many anecdotes are still told. One of these demonstrates something of the independence of character of the grand old man.

One very cold day Rob was rowing a gentleman who hooked a fish. Rob rowed ashore, the fish was landed and the gentleman refreshed himself from his hip flask. This happened three times. On the last occasion, instead of getting back into the boat, Rob sauntered away. The gentleman called out, 'Rob, Rob, where are you going?' Whereupon Rob replied, 'Them that drinks by theirsels, can fish by theirsels', and stomped home.

———————————⊃•⊂———————————

I have some sympathy with Rob of the Trews but none for a certain gillie whose behaviour still angers me whenever I recall it. . ..

'Have ye got any whusky? Because if there's nae whusky, there's nae fush!'

That's was the extraordinary greeting of the head gillie when my husband and I arrived on a famous beat of a Scottish salmon river as guests of a friend who had paid for the beat but was unable to come. We thought it was a poor joke but quickly found that the gillie was serious. Had we hired the beat ourselves we would have been smartly on to the factor to complain. Instead the wretched man got his dram before he even started to put our tackle up.

I went to the car to find my fishing hat and, on returning to the hut, found the gillie pouring himself another dram and spilling quite a lot in the process. 'What do you think you are doing?' I asked angrily.

'Oh, I had a bad night.'

I took the bottle from him, saying, 'Nobody helps himself to my Scotch without being invited.'

Our anger dissipated during the day as we each caught several good fish and the whisky level sank proportionately as the gillie was given the ritual dram after each capture.

On the following day we had two guests, a famous professor and his assistant, who had brought a bottle of the Glenlivet to enliven the day. When the head gillie saw this expensive bottle in the hut he immediately asked if he could sample it and the guest, who was rather non-plussed, poured him a dram. At that moment the under-gillie walked in, whereupon the head gillie remarked, 'Ah, Donald! There's a touch of the Glenlivet here', and to everyone's astonishment poured his colleague a dram with another one for himself.

The same two guests were fishing with us again the next day and the head gillie had the effrontery to ask if the bottle of Glenlivet had been finished. 'No, it's in my car,' the owner answered, whereupon the ever-thirsty man went out of the hut, returned with the bottle and poured himself a large glass.

We were wondering what to do when the laird who owned the beat, and happened to be a friend of ours, decided to join us for a day's fishing himself. It was a very different head gillie who presented himself that day. There was no talk of whusky. Nor, having seen that we were on close terms with the laird and his wife, did he ever take such a liberty again.

Later we asked several previous tenants of the beat if they had been subjected to the same treatment. They all had and they all admitted that they had provided several bottles of whisky in the course of the week because they had travelled a long way and believed that he meant his threat – 'Nae whusky, nae fush!'.

———————◦———————

Fortunately, there are few gillies like that. Most of those I have met have not only been very helpful when fishing has been good but have enlivened the day with their good humour and stories when it has been bad, and this book is much in debt to them. Some are helpful beyond the bounds of duty, as **Captain George Brodrick,** found.

The long hot summer of 1986 was delightful for those on beach holidays but disastrous for salmon fishers. My friend Mark Wrigley and I were among those who had taken beats on the Tweed in the last week in September, when the river was dead low and the pools empty of fish, save for those nearer the mouth which were swarming with salmon waiting for fresh water.

John Taylor, the Duke of Sutherland's gillie for the Upper Mertown beat, confirmed our fears and between us we had only one fish for the week, a small salmon caught on the first morning. There was, however, to be a substantial recompense for the low water.

The bottom pool of the beat is called the Kipper and normally there is a fast and powerful current of some 250 yards before it tails off into quieter and broader water. It was so low that on the Thursday I decided to wade across it below the tail, as I had seen Mark do without much trouble on the previous day. Sadly, I am not as young and rather lame and when I had reached midstream I found things more difficult than I had imagined. The bottom was extremely slippery and I was soon floundering in the current with water pouring into my chest waders and the thong of my wading stick throttling me. After being pushed down some twenty yards or so I managed to scramble out, unhurt but sodden and humiliated.

The following morning, when motoring to the beat, I happened to look at my left hand on the steering wheel and realised that I had lost my lapis lazuli signet ring, which had never left my finger since my wife had given it to me many years before. I was very upset because I knew I must have lost it while thrashing about in the river and that it was probably being trundled down to Berwick.

It was Mark's turn to fish the Kipper with John Taylor and, before I left them, the gillie wanted to know exactly where I had entered the river and where I had left it. I thanked him for his care but assured him that it would be a waste of time looking for the ring.

By 12.30 I was back at the lunch hut drowning my several sorrows in gin and tonic when Mark and the gillie arrived with the inevitable news. 'No fish,' said the gillie, 'but we did strike gold!' He opened his left hand and there, on his finger, was my ring winking in the sunlight.

He then explained how he had found it. He had found the exact point where I had slipped by seeing where the algae on the boulders had been scraped by the soles of my waders. He had then taken what he called 'a slow stroll down the Tweed', staring intently into the current as he waded. About thirty yards below he spotted a glint, waded ashore, stripped to the waist, returned and picked out the ring.

Surely a most remarkable retrieve and a tribute to a professional's knowledge of his river!

———————◦◦———————

It is especially rewarding to catch a fish against a gillie's advice, in a pool which he has deemed to be too high or with a fly he has judged to be too big, and my husband had just such a satisfying experience over several days on the Grimersta fishery on the Island of Lewis.

On arrival at the fishing hut I sought the advice of the gillie concerning flies. He looked at my large selection, which had recently served me well in Iceland, and assured me that I would do no good with any of them. The other guests, who were old stagers, agreed with him but made no offer of smaller patterns.

That evening I browsed through the Grimersta records and saw that in its great days most of the salmon had been caught on very large flies, both in the little river and in the several lochs. I could not believe that the salmon had changed its taking habits so I resolved to continue with my medium-sized patterns.

The sport was hardly furious but in the five days I caught substantially more fish than anyone else and, when I left, some of the rods were cadging larger flies.

George Melly, the writer, jazz-singer and authority on modern art, had a similar, satisfying experience.

I had fished for trout for most of my life but had never had the opportunity to try for a salmon until the mid-1960s when I was invited by a very rich friend to visit Scotland for a couple of days to fish the River Spey. This was something I had never been able to afford and, at the current prices on that river, would find it a considerable strain on my resources even today.

On arrival, I found myself surrounded by retired colonels and hanging judges. The extremely blunt gillie looked contemptuously at my thigh waders and asked me what I did for a living. On discovering that I was a writer he expressed surprise that I could afford the prospect ahead. I explained that I was a guest. 'Aye, that's what I thought,' he said dismissively.

The river was not in ideal condition but, under his tuition, I caught two salmon and a large sea trout. The only other successful angler was a second lieutenant who, in consequence, did not endear himself to his frustrated superior officers. Nor did they take to me. Indeed there was a lot of chuntering after my first fish because I had used a spinner when the legality of such a course was under scrutiny due to the height of the water.

When I caught my second salmon on a fly, on the following day, they were purple with rage but the gillie became infinitely more polite. I have a photograph of myself with the salmon and the sea trout and sometimes I allow myself a small gloat.

I have caught only one salmon since – during a spate on the Usk, where I fish for trout. Sadly, the salmon in the Usk run up mostly in September and October – which happens to be the busiest period of my year.

There are times, of course, when gillies are infuriatingly right, for no reason that seems to make sense. Again, I am grateful to **Captain George Brodrick** for a remarkable example of a gillie's knowledge.

A friend and I had been invited to fish for salmon and sea trout in Loch Carron in Wester Ross by a neighbour in Kent who was an absolute purist, allowing only fly, whatever the conditions. Sadly for us, the conditions were the worst, as our genial host warned us on our arrival after a very long journey – bright sunshine, blue skies, no wind, so not a ripple on the loch. And there was no sign of change.

His forecast was correct. As we set out in separate boats next morning the weather was Mediterranean and everything was beautiful, except for the prospects. My gillie and oarsman, who insisted on wearing his thick tweed suit with waistcoat, offered us no hope as we tried every kind and size of fly.

Eventually I said to him as casually as I could, 'Surely we would have a better chance if we could troll.'

'Maybe,' he replied, 'but you know the Major, he would never let you troll.'

That evening my companion and I induced our host to drink liberally and after the sixth whisky we finally broke him down.

'All right! You've come a long way. I shan't be looking but you can troll.'

Victory! The following morning, a re-run of the first day weather-wise, we went out with hope renewed and a battery of bait boxes containing every kind of lure. I opened them with some flourish but, after careful scrutiny, the gillie pronounced his disheartening opinion – I'm afraid you'll no catch a salmon with anything there.'

I was not prepared to believe him but he was right. Yellowbellies, brown-and-golds, spoons, Tobies – all proved useless and I had to admit defeat.

'Are you sure there are salmon in the loch?' I asked.

'Oh, ay. It's just that you dinna have the necessary.'

'And what might that be?'

'A sandeel'.

I had heard of a sandeel but never seen one.

'Where can we get some for tomorrow?' I asked, excitedly.

'Nowhere,' he said with a shake of the head, as he pulled for the shore.

How we cursed that we had no sandeels when, on the third and last day, we ventured out across that glassy surface.

I had fished for some time and was beginning to feel bored as well as sleepy in the sun when the gillie said, quietly, 'Reel in, sir'.

Having done so I looked up to see him fishing about in his pocket and saw him produce what looked like part of a used condom.

'Now, sir, you'll have your salmon,' he declared, as he proceeded to tie this unattractive object on the end of a trace.

'What on earth is it?' I asked.

'A sandeel'.

Unbelievably, within ten minutes of restarting to troll there was a terrific pull. Gently he rowed me to the bank and, after a fine fight, we grassed a 12-pound fish, as fresh as could be.

Astonished and delighted, I asked the gillie where he had found the sandeel, or part of it, as the gillie said that that was all the bait was.

'Funny thing,' he replied. 'At breakfast time yesterday my wife asked me if I would get her a haddock for our dinner, so I called on one of the fishermen on the way home last evening and got one. When I was cleaning it I found the remains of a sandeel it had eaten. That's what you caught your salmon on. Sadly, it's the only one there is. So you'll be catching no more.'

Once again he was right. We carried on as before until evening without an offer.

What was the sandeel's secret? How could the gillie have been so sure? And how many could we have caught if we had been lucky enough to have had a good supply?

Most gillies are down-to-earth people but, occasionally, an angler encounters one who is so superstitious that nothing will shake his belief. I did so when fishing the Red Gorton beat of the Tay some years ago.

My husband and I had been asked to switch for the day from the South Esk, which we had come to fish, to Red Gorton, and were looking forward to it until, on arrival, we discovered that we were going to be harling. This entailed sitting in a boat and being rowed and motored up and down the river with our rods, with huge plug baits attached, sticking out over the stern. A boring prospect but for one thing – our host had assured us that during the previous week an angler sent on a similar mission had almost filled the boat with large salmon.

Within ten minutes a fresh salmon of about twelve pounds had attached itself to my husband's plug but, when duly landed, the gillie exclaimed, 'I dinna like that.'

Thinking he had done something wrong, my husband asked, 'What don't you like?'

'Catching a fish that quick. We won't get another. You never do when you get one right awa.'

We both thought it was rubbish but avoided saying so. Instead we felt that events would quickly prove the man's stupidity.

Instead they proved his prediction. We fished all day, apart from the lunch break, and while we caught kelt after kelt we never hooked another fresh fish.

Fortunately, the gillie was a Scot of few words and did not say, 'I told you so.'

The habit of a few gillies which has infuriated me is their excessive handiness with the gaff in their determination to get a salmon safely on the bank. On humane grounds, no fish should be played longer than it needs to be but playing a salmon is an essential part of the sport, in my opinion, and the fish should be given a chance to fight for its life and to win, if it is strong and cunning enough.

There was one gillie on the Welsh Dee, near Llangollen, who was a dab hand at gaffing a hooked salmon out before it had properly appreciated its predicament. Whenever an angler remonstrated with him he used to remark:

'They catch cold if you leave them in the water too long!'

There are, of course, occasions when a salmon comes in literally like a log and this happened to me on the Tay. I was so sure it was a log that I handlined it in and found that I was not beaching a bit of sunken wood but a 17-pound salmon.

Later, the gillie, Bob Grant, said to my husband, 'I love looking after your wife: there's never a dull moment!'

Among several stories of this genre sent to me the one most worthy of record concerns what proved to be a world record fish, the raconteur being my son-in-law, **Tony Barron**, an property agent in Sydney.

Round about 1976 I met a keen Australian game fisherman called Norm Smith. I had always wanted to give
game fishing a try and Norm invited me to join the team
on his boat, *Super Screw*, a 23-footer which fished out of
the Port Hacking Game Fishing Club in Sydney.

Fishing days start about 6.30 a.m. The competition
generally begins at 8 a.m. – it takes an hour and a
half to reach the blue-water fishing grounds – with a
closing deadline of 4 p.m. We fished for shark, tuna
or marlin. Of all the sharks, the mako is the only one
that earns big competition points, as it is the only one
of the breed that leaps from the water like a marlin.

The weather was warm with light breezes and a
medium swell. We had fished for more than three hours,
pulping up old tuna to attract the quarry. We had two
set lines from the back of the boat, one of 12-pound
breaking strain, the other of 25. Each had a wire trace,
a large stainless steel shark hook and a 2-kilogram tuna
bait. Each line was supported by a disposable float, an
empty detergent bottle tied on by a small piece of cotton
which would break if a fish took the bait.

Suddenly a shark surfaced a hundred yards behind
the boat and circled the bait. He took on the 12-pound
line and dived. He could not be held and broke the line.
The shark then resurfaced and swam back towards the
boat. He was a big mako, about ten feet long, and as he
swam alongside we could see the trace still in his mouth.

Another bait was prepared, rigged up and tossed over-
board but, in the haste, the line, which should have been
25-pound, was only 6-pound! Inevitably, our mako, the
same fish, took the new bait on the light line. Obviously
it could not be held but as it swam alongside the boat
again one of the crew got a gaff into it and before the
huge fish quite realised what was happening there were
several gaffs in it and a rope round its tail.

We then made our way back to the club, towing the
shark because makos, being extremely dangerous and
not always as dead as they seem, are never brought

on board. It weighed in at 342 pounds and, on 6-pound line, was a world record, registered with the International Game Fishing Association in Florida under the name of Norm Smith. It may still stand as a record but none of us was particularly proud of gaffing a green fish.

The 6-pound line recalls an unusual story from **Charles Oliver-Bellasis**, a keen sportsman who assists in running the family estate in Hampshire.

I was fishing the famous Vanstone beat of the Wye and had arrived there without my spools of nylon for making the trace for my fly. There was always a chance of a big fish and, because the beat was weedy, I would have used 20-pound breaking strain but all the gillie had to offer was of 6-pound strength. He assured me that it would be sufficient since only grilse could be expected.

The day was dull until about 4 p.m., when fish began to show as a small run entered the pool. In short order I was into a big salmon which I saw several times clearly enough to put its weight at probably just under twenty pounds. I did my best to keep it out of the weeds but failed and, once installed there, it quickly broke the trace.

Naturally, I was deeply disappointed and was, I suppose, blaming the gillie for producing such fine nylon when the blame really lay with myself for forgetting to bring the spools. I was, perhaps, a bit curt with him when he asked, 'What sex do you think that fish was, sir?'

'Good God, I've never been asked that before,' I replied, 'but if you want to know I'm pretty sure it was a hen fish.'

'Then there's nothing lost, sir, he said.

'How come, nothing lost?' I asked, thinking about that splendid fish of which I was still feeling deeply deprived.

'Oh, we always put hen fish back in September. At least, rods are encouraged to.'

I discovered that he was speaking the truth and felt much better. 'Good luck to her,' I thought. 'Let's hope I return in a few years' time and catch some of her offspring.'

Perhaps in these days of shortage of wild salmon we should all put more salmon back, especially if they are red and not really fit to eat. I have to admit that I have not yet done so, if only because the riparian owners want the fish in their record books as the number of fish caught per annum decides the capital value of their beats. Still, a fish could be weighed and returned and still entered in the books – which should certainly have happened to a monster caught on the Tay by my husband, **Harry Chapman Pincher.**

In the billiard room of Kinnaird House, near Dunkeld, there is an array of stuffed salmon, all over forty pounds, caught on the Kinnaird beat or on beats lower down by members of the Ward family. Their common feature was that in addition to being long they were also very deep and fat right down to the tail. So many years had passed since the capture of such a monster that I hoped, in the unlikely event that I might catch one, that the owner might agree to set it up in one of the blank spaces still remaining.

While fishing at Kinnaird with the estimable Bob Grant as gillie in October 1987, when the wretched commercial nets had been removed to allow a few fish upstream to spawn, I hooked a very large salmon on a Toby. My spirits soared as I saw it turn on its side. It was as long and as deep as any in the glass cases. After a dour struggle in fast water I eventually brought the fish in close enough for Bob to gaff it and as it came out I felt sure that my first forty-pounder was on the bank. Sadly it was not to be.

'Blast! It's a razor-back,' Bob declared as he administered the priest. I had not heard of such a beast but Bob quickly showed what he meant by running his finger along the fish's back. The backbone showed all the way along.

When we returned to the house we showed the fish sideways on through the window and the other rods came running out to see the monster which, it was generally agreed, must have weighed 40 pounds when it had entered the river but only scaled 28.

We had it smoked and it was inedible. How much wiser it would have been to have returned it so that it could have spawned and passed on its genes for gigantism.

One can learn many things from gillies and not just about fishing. I had often wondered why so many Scotsmen, including many gillies, are called Sandy. I had assumed, correctly, that it was short for Alexander, but why should Scotsmen be called after a Greek king? There has been no historical connection between Scotland and Greece as there was with France.

Several academics failed me but a gillie, called Sandy, knew the answer. Way back, Scotland was ruled by three great kings, all called Alexander, after Alexander the Great – a fitting name for any king. In their day these kings were so revered that children were named after them and the tradition continues.

It is not surprising that gillies are knowledgeable for they are asked to do many strange things, none stranger than that recounted by **Sir Denis Mountain**, formerly chairman of the Eagle Star Assurance Company and owner of the incomparable Delfur beat on the Spey.

A long-standing tenant of the Delfur water had left instructions in his will that his ashes were to be scattered in the Otter pool, which had given him great sport. Duly, on a cold and snowy morning in March, in the 1970s, the urn was brought to the pool.

The deceased's regular gillie was to perform the ceremony, which was attended by three other gillies, the officiating clergyman and a few friends. They were suitably dressed for the occasion in dark suits and bowler hats, some of great antiquity.

The grassy bank of the Otter pool is rather steep and as the gillie was respectfully moving down to the water's edge he slipped. Both he and the urn went into the Spey, the urn and his bowler hat floating fast down the stream. As the gillie surfaced he was heard to mutter, 'Oh, my God, my God, mercy, aye! The urn and my hat's awa!'

Obviously, there are things one should not ask a gillie to do and one of them is to interrupt his hard-earned lunch, his 'piece', as **Lord Jock Bruce-Gardyne** discovered.

I was fishing down the immensely long Dipple pool on the Spey many years ago. It was 1 p.m.: lunch time. I could see the rest of the party gathering for lunch by the hut about half a mile up river. One last cast. A rise. Another cast for luck. Another rise. So one more try. This time the salmon took.

I immediately realised I would need help. I was standing on top of a steep rock bank, with a burn coming in immediately to my left. I yelled for help and, eventually, the luncheon party saw that I was into a fish. The gillie was dispatched to help. He was an elderly gentleman and not to be lightly disturbed from the consumption of his 'piece', as gillies called their lunch in those days.

He arrived with a face of thunder, marched straight into the river below me and started waving the net at the fish. 'Reel in, reel in!' he growled. I said that the fish was by no means ready for the net yet. Unfortunately, at this point it chose to move in closer to the rocks. The gillie promptly made a dive for it with the net, caught the cast and that was that.

Without a word he set off back up the bank for the lunch hut with me following, having collected my gear.

When I reached the luncheon party they told me that the gillie had informed them that 'It was not the gentleman playing the fish: it was the fish playing the gentleman'.

The moral of the story is that you come between a gillie and his 'piece' at your peril.

Interference between a gillie and his rod would also seem to be unwise, or at least unwelcome, as **Lord Bruce-Gardyne** also learned.

My first-ever expedition for salmon, which initiated me into the ways and wiles of gillies, was a visit to a spate river in the Hebrides. My friends and I fished two beats with an intervening beat being fished by others. Making my way down from the upper beat to the lower one morning, I found an elderly gentleman standing on the bank of the middle beat with his line caught in a tree behind him. A gillie was sitting further down the bank swatting midges.

I reckoned that it was time for my good deed for the day. Putting down my rod I climbed up into the tree and extricated the line. There was no fly on the end and I pointed this out to the angler. He thanked me and I resumed my journey downstream.

As I passed the gillie he rose and followed me. 'There was no call to tell the shentleman he has nae flee,' he said. 'We're having enough trouble as it is.'

Perhaps the gillie was just exercising his sense of humour in that dour but entertaining way of so many Scottish gillies. The following example has been vouched for by **Anthony Bone**, a businessman who has a special connection with the sporting world through supplying high-class shotguns and sporting pictures.

Ken Oliver, a wonderful sporting gentleman, now gone from us, was fishing with his lifelong friend Terry Wedge on the Lower Floors beat of the Tweed. It was known that the laird's wife, the Duchess of Roxburghe, was expecting a child at any time and when the Duke's gillie, Charlie, appeared one morning Ken asked, 'How is Her Grace?'

'Och, just fine, sir. She kelted last night.'

I suspect that the Irish gillie attending **Admiral of the Fleet Sir Henry Leach** was also practising his brand of tact and humour.

Tall and slim, he was a quiet-spoken man whose faded blue eyes told of much rock, heather, sun and rain. His speech was slow like his movements. After all, what was the point of hassle and hurry when you had all the time in the world? But he like to be back at his cottage by six o'clock of an evening to milk his one cow. Like many real

countrymen his attitude could be summed up in a word
– gentle.

Peter Ridge was a bachelor and a gillie. He and a
small regiment of brothers and cousins lived at Cashel, a
tiny village on the west coast of Connemara, overlooking
Galway Bay. Peter never boasted that he knew where the
fish would be lying but quietly rowed you to that part of
the lough from which he judged it best to start your drift.
Usually he was right. He was also an optimist who always
liked to be encouraging.

One August morning in 1958 it was overcast with
heavy, low clouds scudding across the sky before a
stiff northerly breeze. A thin drizzle was falling and
conditions seemed good for fishing except for the wind
blowing from the north.

'What do you think of it, Peter?' I asked the oracle.

'Well, perhaps the fish would take if the wind was all
right.'

And what do you make of the wind?'

'Ay, the wind. . . .' He looked pensively skywards. 'The
wind is from the north but maybe there's a touch of the
south in it.'

Stories about Irish gillies are legion, and many are
apocryphal, but my friend and neighbour **Joan Hirsch**
vouches for the truth of the next.

Some friends of my late husband, Jack Hirsch, joined
him at Ballyhooly on the Blackwater for a week's fishing
in 1923, when he was a young soldier and during the
time of the 'troubles'. On their first day they happened to
overhear the gillies talking among themselves and were
horrified.

'And what will you be doing next week?' one asked.

'Next Tuesday we're going to kill Kelly.'

71

'Are you now? Well, that very same day we're going to kill Michael and at the end of the week we are going to kill Mare.'

Kilkelly is a place in Mayo, while Kilmichael and Kilmare are in Wexford.

The visitors left for England the next day!

As most gillies will tell you, given half a chance, they have to put up with some peculiar anglers and do it with good grace. But there are occasions when their patience and their tempers are frayed beyond limit. My husband has confessed to causing such a situation in a story which he has entitled 'Putting up a Black with Brown'.

One of the most famed gillies on the Aberdeenshire Dee (after whom a pool is named) was called Frank Brown. He was also one of the most dour and is credited with a much retailed remark. Late one Saturday afternoon, an angler who had rented his beat caught his only salmon and looking down on it said, 'Brown, that fish has cost me £100' – that being the quite expensive rent in those days. Brown's only response was 'It's a guid thing, then, that ye didn'a get two!' Sadly it was against Brown that I committed my gravest offence against a gillie and I shall never forget his face when he realised what I had done.

I was fishing the Blackhall beat shortly after the end of the Second World War as a guest of an extraordinary Aberdeen fish-dealer called Joe Little, a tough but generous and most amusing man who had originally hailed from Hull. I had done very little salmon fishing and was using one of the very first glass-fibre spinning rods which had been sent to me by the manufacturers in the hope that I would give it some publicity. We had all caught fish and were due to stop fishing early enough

to go to the theatre in Aberdeen when I hooked what appeared to be a large salmon. Brown cried that I was being too gentle with it and, responding to a demand from Joe to 'Give it some bloody lardy', I did my best and the rod snapped at the butt like a carrot. I then proceeded to play the fish, which was doing what it liked on the other side of the river, holding the severed part of the rod while a friend had the butt with the reel.

I was making no progress as darkness began to fall but was determined to get the fish, which none of us had yet seen. Eventually, when time was really running out and the light was fading fast, we managed to get the fish into the side, where Brown expertly whipped his gaff into it and slung it onto the bank.

'It's a bloody kelt!' he cried in horror.

Indeed it was a kelt – about fifteen pounds and foul-hooked in the back.

It was an unpardonable professional sin to gaff a kelt and a legal offence to kill one. Worse still, three other gillies had seen him do it and could hardly be expected to keep quiet about it.

Relations between myself and Brown were never cordial again and I could not blame him. He would have been much less insulted had I hooked him in the face.

Gillies, of course, put up their own share of 'blacks' with rods and my friend, **Cavaliere del Lavoro Massimo Coen**, sent me an intriguing example.

It was August on the Italian–Austrian frontier. The high peaks in the Dolomites still bore snow. From a mountain lake set among pine trees, the Lake of Anterselva, a lovely river flowed towards Brunico. I had been invited by a colleague to fish in this jealously guarded preserve,

which used to be the property of Enrico Mattei, the crea-
tor of the Italian petrol industry and one of the makers
of the Italian 'economic miracle'.

After three days of fishing in this paradise, sixteen trout
had already been landed on the dry fly. We were coming
to the end and the time had passed in a flash.

The gillie, who spoke both Italian and German, had
become quite friendly. We talked about Kurt Waldheim. I
told him that I could not stomach the fact that he had been
in the SS. The gillie seemed to agree with my sentiments
and then remarked, 'I was in the SS myself.' I was stunned
and appalled. Coen and the SS are not a happy mixture.

The fact that the gillie said that he had been put into
the SS when he was only eighteen at the end of the
war helped a little but, with that one remark, the magic
seemed to have gone out of the trip. Then the last trout
took and my fury was discharged as I landed it.

I looked at the snowy mountains, the glittering lake
and the pines darkened by the failing light. Oh to hell!
Politics and fishing do not mix. Let's go home.

I felt almost the same way about a gillie on the Dee who
came down to our beat – one that we had never fished
before and never did again – in search of a floating fly
line which had been lost by one of his rods higher up
the river. No fish had been involved yet, somehow, the
angler's backing had snapped when all his line was out.

The gillie passed the time of day with my husband and
they commiserated on the lack of fish, for both beats had
been blank so far that week.

'Never mind,' he said. 'The weather's nice. You know,
these days you should regard coming here as a holiday
and if you get a fish it's a bonus.'

When I thought of the cost of the beat, the tackle, and
the hotel, as well as all the trouble of getting there, I was
appalled at such an admission. But, sadly, I fear he was
right.

FISHY BUSINESS

A lost line is not uncommon; the loss of the whole outfit, as witnessed by my husband, must count as an exceptional event.

Shortly after the end of the Second World War, the latest-technology spinning rods were made of tubular steel and fitted with multiplying reels. The casting technique was to put the shortish rod over the shoulder and project the bait forwards and high into the air. If the reel was expertly thumbed to avoid birds'-nests, long and accurate casts could be made.

At that time I rented a most exciting and beautiful lake in Hampshire which contained some very large pike. Among the guests I took there was my Fleet Street colleague, Basil Cardew, the air correspondent of the *Daily Express*, who had just taken up fishing, with my encouragement.

One lovely autumn day Basil and I were casting away with plugs from the same drifting boat when, seeing a swirl some distance off, he essayed a mighty cast. Regrettably, he let go of the rod and the whole apparatus sailed into the air in a neat parabola, entering the lake some distance away from the boat in one of the deepest parts. I wanted to fish for the line immediately with a weighted spoon but Basil was more concerned about the embarrassment of what he had done than with his loss. Another couple of friends were fishing in a boat not far away and, as they had not seen the event, he did not want them to know about it.

He had already decided what he would do. He would borrow a large magnet from one of the aircraft manufacturers he was associated with in his work, and, on the following weekend, we could come down again, fasten the magnet to a rope and bobble it over the bottom until it attracted the steel rod. It sounded an unlikely eventuality but he was confident, so we marked the spot where he thought the rod had landed, lining it up with certain trees.

The following weekend we duly arrived and, with some

80

flourish, he produced the equipment which friends had provided from the boot of his car. The magnet was not only expensively high-tech, being made of some alloy, not iron, but so huge that it needed a heavy rope to ensure that it would not break off and also be lost in the deep.

All was made ready for the hunt but, regrettably, Basil dropped the magnet on concrete in the boat-house and it shattered. What might remain of the rod, reel, nylon line and the bait is still there to this day.

———————————>●<———————————

A rather more successful recovery was achieved by the late Sir Brian Mountain, as his son, **Sir Denis**, remembers.

During a very large spate on the Delfur water of the River Spey my brother borrowed a spinning rod and fitted it with a brand-new multiplier reel which the local doctor had left, probably in error, in the fishing-room cupboard in our house. With an almighty swing he hurled the bait across the river and was left with only the short butt extension in his hand.

Three days later my father was boating in the pool below and hooked a fish on the fly. After a considerable struggle, he and the gillie realised that the fish was snagged. Letting the boat down on a rope fixed to an anchor, they managed to gaff the fish, which was tangled in a nylon line. With the fish in the boat and the line in their hands they managed to free the bait attached to it from the riverbed and, pulling in more line as they moved downstream, they recovered both the missing rod and the reel. The rod had gone white but the reel and line were undamaged.

On Speyside news may travel slowly but it gets there. That evening the doctor called at the house to say that he had heard that his reel had been lost.

'What reel?' my brother asked.

'The one I left in the fishing-room cupboard.'

'Well, if you were foolish enough to leave it there I am sure that if we have a look it will still be there.'

The doctor went off with his reel, no doubt intending to have a harsh word with the source of his false information. If he reads this perhaps he will have to apologise!

The foul-hooked fish is a major source of fishing tales and some of those which are unquestionably true are quite astonishing in terms of the laws of chance. The first of several I have selected comes from **Peter Spence**, a land and river owner.

In April 1985 a Belgian guest was fishing the Bothy pool of the Carron beat of the River Spey using a large silver spoon in high water. He hooked and lost a salmon which had been lying in the second swirl down from the point. Examination indicated that the knot of the nylon trace to the spoon had been faulty.

Returning to the same pool two days later, the Belgian, then fishing with a 2-inch wooden Devon minnow, hooked and landed a ten-pound fish from the same swirl. The fish had not taken his bait. By chance one of the treble hooks on the Devon had inserted itself into the eye of the swivel of the large spoon which was protruding from the salmon's mouth. It was the spoon – and the fish – which the angler had lost two days earlier.

My husband is the source of the next 'unlucky salmon' story.

While I was fishing the Blackhall beat of the Aberdeenshire Dee as a guest of Mr Jock Leslie, his son, then aged about seventeen, hooked a large salmon while spinning in the neck of the Roe Pot pool in fairly high spring water. He was using a golden sprat – then the standard bait – mounted in a transparent plastic device which had a large stiff loop to which the nylon trace was fastened. After a few seconds the line came back without the bait and the youth was soundly – and rightly – berated by his father for having tied a faulty knot.

Having been shown the knotting technique once again, the boy cast the bait into the same place and hooked a large springer, which he played successfully and which, I believe, weighed 22 pounds. The fish was the one he had already hooked and the treble of the second bait had chanced to slide into the loop of the golden sprat protruding from its mouth.

Major General Sir John Acland, now a farmer and company director, contributes the third example under the title 'Rodeo on the Naver'.

A year or two ago, on 29 July, my wife and I were fishing near the top of the River Naver in the very north of Scotland. She had already caught two fish whereas I had succeeded only in losing one. Shortly after she had left with the gillie, the legendary Tommy Shaw, to fish a tiny pool named the Crack, I hooked a fish – a big one for the Naver – and, after playing it for twenty minutes or more, had it almost in the net. At that point it came off and as it did so I became aware of Tommy, with my wife, coming down the river carrying her third fish. My pleasure at this success was a little soured by the thought that I had just lost a fish which was, perhaps, as big as her three put together.

We moved down to Brown's pool, where Tommy suggested I should dap the fast stream. He and my wife remained on the high bank, giving the appearance of being a little self-satisfied. About halfway down the pool I hooked a fish on the tail fly. After playing it for a minute or two and seeing that it was of no great size, I was aware of Tommy descending the bank with his net. 'Don't bother,' I called to him. 'It will be off in a minute.' Sure enough, it was.

I began to wade back to the bank when I became aware that there was something attached to my line. I started to reel in and whatever it was came lightly and unresistingly towards me. As it came in we saw that it was a six-pound salmon, lassoed round the gills with a double turn of the cast held firm by the dropper and the tail fly hooked together. From the small fresh wound in its mouth it was clear that it was the fish I had originally hooked. The lasso had, apparently, prevented the gills from working and drowned the fish. All that Tommy said was, 'Well, your wife hasn't got one like that yet.'

The following year, on the same river and the same day, I was fishing the Wall, a curiously formed pool with a deep, narrow stream against the far bank. Few fish were showing, though my wife had caught three while I remained blank. I started with surprise when an obviously fresh fish suddenly leapt from the water only about twelve yards from me and roughly where my fly must be. It seemed to ascend to about five feet in a convulsive corkscrew motion before crashing back into the water. I had never seen a fish behave quite like that before and, as I wondered what the cause was, I became aware that it was, in fact, attached to my line. This became more evident as it careered downstream for the better part of a hundred yards.

I followed it and, in a wider, quieter pool, it proceeded to rush back and forth for several minutes. By this time Tommy had come down and joined me and we agreed that it must be foul-hooked. There was a long, shallow, pebbly stretch of water running to the edge of the pool and we thought it would be best to beach the fish. By this time it was almost finished and, after a little while longer I began to draw it in. To our surprise it came in tail first and we saw that it was firmly lassoed round the tail, one hook of the tiny treble having caught round the cast.

Later we were joined by some friends, one of whom, having heard the tale, said to Tommy, 'Surely it must be impossible to lasso a salmon!' With no more than a vestige of an eye-twinkle, he replied, 'Ay, but the General will do almost anything to get a fish when his wife's a wee bit ahead of him.'

Those fish were caught by what seems a chance in a million, or several millions. Having three different kinds of fish take on a single cast, as happened to **Sir Denis Mountain**, must be even rarer.

The Spey is renowned for its large brown trout as well as for its salmon. Fishing with a dropper fly in a tiny backwater off a very fast-flowing stretch of the river, it was often possible to take a large brownie, so long as one crawled over the stones and bobbled the dropper on the surface. On one occasion as soon as I began to bobble the fly I saw it taken by a nice brownie of about three pounds.

Playing such a fish was always difficult because if it got into the fast water there was no way of getting it back and no way to follow it down. As I always did in that place, I held on and took the fish round and round the backwater. The fish refused to tire but after a long battle it gave in. It was not the brownie which I had seen take the dropper but a sea trout of about two pounds and on the tail fly was a grilse. I netted both of them.

I can only assume that the grilse took the tail fly while the brownie was being played, and that in the ensuing melée the brownie slipped the hook, which was taken later by the sea trout.

————————◦◦◦————————

John Bridgeman's tale is even more remarkable.

It must be rare for a salmon hooked on a short spinning rod to be eventually landed by the same angler fishing with a long fly rod, but that was the experience which befell me while fishing the River Driva in Norway in 1959. I was spinning down a long, deep pool from the bank, with Ivar, the gillie, following me and carrying my fly rod. I was soon into a salmon, which headed straight for the rapids below. While I was wondering if I could hold him, the backing parted from the plaited nylon spinning line and I was left to reflect that I had lost not only a fine fish but 50 yards of line.

Seizing my fly rod, I set off for the next pool some 400 yards downstream, where Ivar and I got into a boat and moved out towards the main stream, which at that point hugged the far bank. I kept looking into the water for my line and, as we were returning to our own bank, Ivar yelled as he spotted the white spinning line lying on the bottom in fairly shallow water. We fished it up and tied it to the end of my fly line.

Ivar rowed me out as I reeled in the slack only to find that the line was hard round a rock. By skilful manoeuvring he freed the line and we followed out into the stronger water, where it was round yet another rock. With great difficulty he freed it again and, to my delight, the reel began to scream and I was playing the salmon again – this time on a fly rod and from a boat in which I could follow the fish.

After I had played him for ten minutes he made a dash for the tail of the pool and we followed him down the rapids to an island, where I clambered out and eventually landed him – a fresh-run 25-pounder hooked in the dorsal fin.

Gerald Ward, a Wiltshire landowner and extra equerry to the Prince of Wales, witnessed an even more bizarre instance.

A guest on the Kinnaird beat of the Tay, bait-fishing the Ash Tree pool which is noted for holding big salmon, had been playing a fish for several minutes when the line parted. To drown their sorrows the angler and his companion stopped fishing for a drink and a rest.

Half an hour later, the man then in charge of river, aptly called Gillies, returned to the pool and saw a line being towed across the surface of the water, which is exceptionally deep. He was carrying a bait rod and with speed, accuracy and luck cast across the line, snagged it and began to play the fish. As the lunch hut was nearby a small crowd gathered to watch. There was every chance that the bait would slip from the line, but fortunately the current had contorted the line into a bit of a bird's-nest and he beached the fish to loud cheers from the other side. Of all the fish he had caught and seen caught this was the one he remembered best. The original angler even got his bait back.

Occasionally two rods become involved in the playing of a single fish. **Sam Nickerson,** of the Nickerson farming and seed merchants family, a wonderful shot and keen fisherman, contributes the following account.

My wife, Connie, was spinning in front of the hut on the

Banchory Lodge Hotel water on the Dee, and hooked a salmon which took out a lot of line and rushed to the other side of the river, which is wide there. Another angler was spinning from the other side and the salmon fouled his line. He could not disengage his line, so what was to be done?

As the fish was on his side of the river he called to my wife to slacken her line and let him play the fish, though, had I been there, I would have suggested the reverse. Fortunately his gambit worked and, though it took a long time, he eventually gaffed a fresh-run ten-pounder. It had not been foul-hooked but it had been foul-played.

There was no argument as to the ownership of that fish. Once it was on the bank it belonged to the angler who had hooked it and had maintained contact. But in the circumstances of the following, much more remarkable story, contributed by **Peter Spence**, the question remained in considerable doubt.

The Awe is a very turbulent, fast-flowing river littered with large boulders of every size and shape. It was once noted for its monster salmon and, though these are much rarer now, they do occur. In August 1986, while fly-fishing from the left bank of the Colonel's pool at 3 p.m., my friend Michael Gatehouse hooked a large fish which, by 3.30, was sulking in its original lie, totally unwilling to move. As I had arrived on the opposite bank, Michael shouted for advice and several gambits were tried – pressure upstream, pressure downstream, pumping and bombardment with rocks – all to no avail. If he wasn't stuck in the bottom, which I had begun to suspect, Michael was going to be there all night.

Remembering the advice of my venerable father, I suggested that I should take off my fly and attach a size 14 treble and, casting from my bank, catch his line to exert pressure from a different angle. This worked. The fish shot up the pool, I flicked off my treble but the fish returned to its lie to sulk again. I repeated this three times and always the fish moved and returned to its lie. At the fourth attempt my treble slid down the line and became hooked into the fish, which was now on two lines on opposite sides of the river.

The salmon then set off for the Red Rock pool below, managing to foul Michael's line round a large boulder in the process. While I was able to run with the fish, which was now on my side of the water, Michael was losing more and more line and backing wrapped round rocks. For the next two hours the fish was never more than six or seven yards from me.

I battled from one rock to another all the way down the rapids between Red Rock and the Shepherd's pool, while Michael was some 200 yards upstream playing the rocks. It did not help that it was pouring with rain.

The fish was incredibly powerful and with the weight of the water I was unable to control it as it dropped back down the Shepherd's through Watty's Stone, down into Woodrow's pool. Michael was now out of sight and the fishermen who were engaged in these pools were not prepared to accept my explanation of why I was poaching their water. Finally I managed to persuade them that I needed a gillie, or preferably two.

By that time Michael had convinced himself that he had parted company with the fish and after a record-breaking drive over the Awe bridge he, a friend and their wives arrived to see the salmon going down the Meal pool towards the rapids. Large nets were produced and I was able to hold the fish briefly on the surface for it to be netted. The time was 6.21 p.m.

The salmon was a cock fish weighing only 27 pounds but was very thin and must have weighed at least 35 when it had entered the river. My little hook was embedded in its large kype.

I still marvel at the power and determination of that fish and the skill with which it had used the current and the rocks. But whose was it? And had it been fairly caught?

———————

Twenty-seven pounds of salmon in rough water is a heavy load, but what about seventy-seven pounds, a feat described by **Sir Denis Mountain**?

There is a pool on the Alta river in northern Norway called Sierra. The neck of the pool is about seventy-five yards long with fast-flowing and fairly deep water under the right bank, while on the left bank there is an extremely deep back-eddy. The angler is canoed over the eddy to fish the fast water and if he hooks a fish he is rowed back and put ashore.

A Norwegian angler played a fish in this backwater and simply could not bring it in. As the salmon, when hooked, had not seemed inordinately large for the Alta, the puzzled gillie looked into the deep water and saw a huge fish in some kind of distress. He gaffed it and pulled out a 51-pounder with the angler's fly-line lassoed round its tail. He released the line and the rod then landed the 26-pounder which had taken his fly.

———————

That monster was quite out of luck, and sheer ill fortune seems to be yet another of the multitude of hazards which a salmon faces in its long swim to its spawning grounds, as witness this incident recalled by **Bernard Aldrich**.

I have had some odd experiences while managing the salmon and trout fishery at Broadlands, where I have worked for thirty-three years, currently for Lord Romsey and before that for Earl Mountbatten. One day I was walking up the river with old Walter Geary, my predecessor who taught me rivercraft – I was a Londoner and knew nothing when I started – when we saw a salmon roll over and disappear into a pool. I took little notice until Walter saw it roll over again further downstream and said, emphatically, 'That fish is sick. We should get it out.'

As we turned and walked towards it we saw it roll over again and make for the side. It was lying there when we arrived and I had no difficulty in gaffing it out. To our astonishment, it was a perfectly fresh fish, a trifle slim but with sea lice on it. We could not understand what was wrong with it until we saw a pronounced hook mark in the scissors of the jaw. We assumed that it had been played almost to exhaustion and had then got off.

As we walked back to the fishing hut carrying the salmon we met a charming doctor and his wife, regular guests, who had been fishing that morning.

'Any luck, Doctor?' Walter asked.

'I hooked a fish in Cowman's pool and managed to tail it but when I laid it on the bank it looked so like a kelt that I put it back.'

This was the fish we had, all right. And no kelt has sea lice, which the good doctor had missed in giving it the benefit of the doubt.

We handed the fish to its original captor. It must have been one of the unluckiest salmon ever to get that far up the river. I suppose, strictly speaking, that we had poached it but Walter, who was rarely wrong about such things, was sure it would have died anyway. The fight and the brief sojourn on the bank had exhausted it beyond recovery.

There is a lesson for all anglers in this story. When putting back a fish, and especially a large one, hold it in the water head upstream unti it is fully recovered, otherwise it will be tumbled downstream and will literally drown for lack of oxygen.

Many a salmon, lying in the side for one reason or another, has been gaffed out and my husband confesses to having done it once, though inadvertently.

I was fishing the Goyle pool on the Kinnaird beat of the South Esk, near Brechin, and played a large fish which, when exhausted and on a very short line, took refuge under a ledge on which I was standing. I could see the fish's tail so I carefully put the gaff into the water and brought it up smartly. There was a large salmon on the gaff but it was not the one on the end of my line. The pool was so packed with fish waiting to go up the fish ladder there that I had gaffed another which was sheltering under the ledge.

I suppose that having finally grassed the salmon on my line I should have returned it to make up for the one I had 'poached'. I regret to admit that I did not. In those days the supply of salmon seemed limitless.

Professor R. V. Jones, author of *Most Secret War*, records how angling can test human integrity to its limits, especially when fish are few.

I have heard of eminent purists being driven to the prawn on Royal Deeside but I was totally unprepared for the question put to me by the most accomplished and most distinguished angler it has been my privilege to know. He was the late Sir Thomas Merton, Fellow and Treasurer of the Royal Society and one of the greatest connoisseurs of Italian Renaissance art.

We shared an interest in ingenuity of design and the craftsmanship of scientific equipment and we met regularly on various committees. During our talks I learned that he had caught two salmon each over fifty pounds on his own beat of the Wye, which had also produced the largest salmon ever recorded in England.

One evening in his dining room at Maidenhead Thicket, over coffee and port and surrounded by his paintings, which included two Botticellis, he suddenly asked me, 'Have you ever poached a salmon?'

Apart from illicitly shooting a leaping salmon with a pistol, I had not.

'I have,' he announced. 'It's jolly good fun.'

He then told me how it came about. 'It happened one year when my brother and I were in Scotland to fish the Garry near Blair Atholl. The river was very low and the water gin clear. We cast and cast for days but could rise nothing. Then in one cast I felt a pull and when I looked at my fly there was a single salmon scale on the hook. That gave me the idea. The fish were there all right and if we could drag a hook across the pool it might stick in and we would have a chance of catching a fish.'

Realising that a single hook would probably slip over a fish's back he and his brother sat up late that night whipping their single hooks into trebles and weighting them with lead for the next morning. They had reinvented the sniggle with the treble hook, totally unaware that this had been used by poachers for many, many years.

Their success was immediate. 'We kept it up for three days,' Sir Thomas said. 'Our best morning was when we caught twenty-seven. We were giving fish away to everyone who came to watch and we stopped when we feared that the police might catch us. The best fish were the ones that got away.'

I was truly astonished at hearing such a story from this highly civilised and gentle man. We never talked about fishing again.

———————◦———————

That story highlights the predicament which every salmon fisher eventually experiences on occasion even these days – a pool full of fish and not a taker among them. When I am spinning away or putting my fly down a river like the Dee and getting nothing, I put myself in the position of any salmon making its way from the sea upstream. For most of each day, from the moment the fish enters the lowest beat, a bait or a fly is passing its nose. So, I ask myself, why should a fish take mine when it must have ignored thousands of others? It is just a miracle when it happens and, in a way, since the fish is not feeding, it is a suicidal act.

The following tale of an ostensibly suicidal salmon is recounted by the **Duke of Fife**.

My relative, Rivers Bosanquet, was very well named because he was a fanatical freshwater fisherman all his life and took off all the time he could spare from his stockbroking business to pursue the salmon. Normally he was successful but during one whole week on the River Tweed he had fished hard and skilfully without a single rise.

On the Saturday afternoon, after the twentieth 'last cast' which was as unproductive as the thousands which had gone before, he laid down his rod in the boat with a heavy sigh and sat back wearily for the gillie to row him back to the bank – and to dull old stockbroking. When they were almost there a large salmon jumped into the boat and was quickly dispatched by the gillie, no doubt with his tip in mind.

Rivers was considerably cheered for, in one way, it was far better than a fish he might have caught with his last cast. He would be able to dine out on the story for years.

He did, which is why I am able to tell it now.

The late **Ken Robinson** witnessed a similar and, perhaps, more remarkable incident.

Jim Henricks, an American who was keen to become an expert salmon fisher, was watching Ken, who was highly experienced, fishing the Pol Bruaich pool of the Dinnett beat on the Aberdeenshire Dee. Ken hooked a salmon and Jim was so anxious to net it, which he had not done before, that he was allowed to do so. As the fish seemed to be well under control and not more than ten pounds, Ken pointed to a convenient place and said, 'All you have to do is to stand there and hold the net out', meaning in about ten minutes time when the fish would be exhausted. Henricks took him literally and stood at the river's edge holding the net out in front of him some two feet above the water.

Ken was too busy to notice until, after about a minute, the fish decided to come in close where Henricks was standing, made a leap to throw the hook and landed plumb in the dry net.

Jane Hall came across a big sea trout which seemed bent on ending its life, though not in a way to her advantage.

In October 1988 I was fishing for sea trout in Loch Ardlussa on the island of Jura in the Inner Hebrides, at the point where the river runs out of it to the sea. I hooked a good fish on the middle fly and it ran straight

across to the other side of the loch, taking out seventy yards of line and backing and going with such speed and determination that it beached itself.

What does one do in such a situation? A friend had told me that he had cut the backing and then walked round the loch – a long way – hoping to pick up the fish and recover his line but, on arrival, found that the fish had flopped back into the water taking everything with it. I was not going to be caught that way so I decided on the only alternative – to wait, as long as needs be, keeping a moderate strain on the fish.

It took a long time but eventually I saw the fish's tail begin to flip and it rolled back in. After a fight of twenty-five minutes I beached it on the right side. It was just short of seven pounds.

While Jane was telling her story for this book, her husband was reminded of an incident which, while only marginally connected with fishing, is so extraordinary that I cannot resist repeating it.

Richard Hall had gone to a famous sports shop in London in search of a Musto Gore-tex jacket, which would serve for fishing and shooting. He is a large man and the assistant produced the only one in stock likely to fit him. Richard tried it on and, after ensuring that the zips worked, decided to buy it. He could feel something in one of the inside pockets and thinking it must be the instructions unzipped it. He put his hand in and pulled out fifty £50 notes – £2,500 in all!

The assistant, who witnessed the discovery, was embarrassed because it obviously meant that the coat was not entirely new but had been returned by somebody. Possibly it had been loaned to someone for a short time, perhaps for a day's shooting.

The confusion was resolved by the offer of a third reduction in the price. Richard never did hear what happened to the £2,500.

———————◦———————

While many a coarse fish has taken the bait while the angler was dozing, few salmon fishers can have taken a fish that way, but my old Venetian friend **Cavaliere del Lavoro Massimo Coen** admits to having done so.

It was a beautiful day in July on the Bugda in Iceland. Gurgling crystal-clear water meandering through lava fields. I thought I would try the Foss. Nothing. The 15-foot split-cane rod, far too big for the river, was lying on the edge of the bank with the fly dangling in the slack water. I lay down and fell fast asleep in the warm sun.

Suddenly there was a shout. 'The fly is going!' It was my son's friend who was touring Iceland and had joined us for the day.

I jumped up, grabbed the rod and eventually landed a lovely sixteen-pounder, fresh from the sea.

In Italy we say 'Chi dorme non puglia pesci!' – 'He who sleeps does not catch a fish.'

Definitely wrong!

Lord Home of the Hirsel told me that, having been rowed out to fish a pool on the Tweed, he wanted to see how the fly he had selected would look when in the water. He dangled it over the side from his hand and a salmon came up and took it. (He did not say if he caught the fish.)

Those who remember the London businessman, **Peter Adam**, a close and much-missed friend of mine, will know that, keen as he was, he was no great shakes as a salmon fisher. But he could catch fish and one good salmon he took from the Wye virtually committed suicide, according to his daughter Nicky, who witnessed it. Peter made a terrible fly cast into a stream with the cast and line falling close into the side below him like a plate of mince. Nevertheless, a salmon surged in from the pool, found the fly in the tangle and hooked itself.

A similar incident befell my husband while he was fishing the Dee in February, when it was so cold that those great pancakes of soft ice, known locally as grue, were floating down, almost covering the river. As the water was really unfishable the other rods had decided to go shopping in Aberdeen but my husband fished on, occasionally managing to get his bait between the pancakes. Nothing happened until it landed smack on top of a small piece of grue. A salmon rose, took the bait – a golden sprat – off the grue and was hooked and landed. Persistence pays!

Fishing is a sport which lends itself to practical jokes, unlike shooting, where the dangers make such flippancy unacceptable. Some good ones have come my way from friends, like this story from **Sir Michael Hordern**.

March 1st 1987 was as cold a day as ever found me on a river bank. I had been a guest at the annual dinner of the North Devon branch of the Salmon and Trout Association the night before, and my hosts for the evening had been Group Captain Peter and Mrs Norton Smith, who have some two miles of the Torridge and were determined to open the salmon season in style. They assembled a party of some six or eight of us, all slightly 'morning after'. Along with my host and hostess, the party contained James Ferguson, Dermot Wilson and Ted Hughes, the Poet Laureate, among other fishing 'names'.

On arrival at the river we found it very low and iced over from bank to bank except for a few runs where the ice had not quite met in midstream. Generously I was put onto one of these more or less open runs. I was enjoying fishing down it, dropping my fly just off the leading edge of the opposite ice but quite certain in my mind that no salmon was going to take. Peter called out to ask if I would mind if Ted got in at the head of the run and fished down behind me. Of course I didn't.

No sooner had he crouched out over the bank-side ice than there was a shout and, turning, I saw Ted out in the middle of the river, rod bent double, quite certainly into a fish. I could hardly believe my eyes.

'Come and play the fish,' they called to me. Generously meant, of course, but quite against my principles. However, I agreed to act as gillie and land it. Net in hand, I waded out to where the action seemed to be. The salmon seemed to be behaving a bit oddly and I called out to say that I thought it might be foul-hooked but that it looked to be a fresh fish. I could see it, beautifully blue and silver in the ice-clear water. Ultimately, Ted managed to get its head up and I slid the net under it and safely carried it over the ice to the bank, where I put it down on the shingle. The incredible first fish on the first morning of the season – firmly hooked in the scissors!

On putting my hand into the net I discovered that the fish was frozen absolutely solid, as well it might be, having spent the last six months in Ted's freezer. I have to admit that for a split second or two as I handled the fish I marvelled that the cold had been all that intense. Then I appreciated the almost total success of the plot.

In retrospect I had to feel sorry that my principles had spoiled the pleasure which the party would have enjoyed had I been persuaded to take over the rod.

The Laureate has celebrated his catch in a narrative poem of some dozen verses. I seriously doubt that it will find its place in his collected works but it's a treasured possession to remind me of the coldest day on which I have ever fished, of a delicious lunch in the fishing hut

– hot cassoulet and burgundy – and such a gigantic and successful leg-pull.

The late **Jack Block**, who owned several hotels and game parks in Kenya, and was a member of the syndicate on the River Grimersta, was an inveterate practical joker and found the puncturing of pomposity irresistible. A wonderfully generous host, he had offered to put on a day's big-game fishing for a visiting American who, on the preceding evening had been unbearably boastful about his successes off his native shores.

The lines were out, the several rods mounted and, with the boat moving at trolling speed, the fishermen were having a drink in the shade. Jack's boatman shouted that the American's rod had a strike and he emerged to see his line running out fast. He seized the rod excitedly and was strapped into the chair to play it. It looked like a good fish because whatever he did it refused to come in and kept taking more and more line. After half an hour or so the American was so exhausted that he was permitted to haul in his prize. It was a large canvas bucket which Jack had arranged to have fixed to his line. Jack had taken the wheel and, having played the trick before, was expert at it. Whenever his guest looked like making headway in reeling in the line he simply made the boat go faster and could make the bucket 'play' by slightly swerving the boat from side to side.

Happily, the American appreciated the joke and joined in the laughter.

Not long afterwards poor Jack was drowned while fishing in a mountain stream in Chile.

Such jokes can, of course, go wrong and rebound on the perpetrator, as **Sir Donald Gosling** describes.

I had taken a small party of anglers out in a boat off the south coast and we had not been fishing long when the wind increased in strength and the sea became very choppy. One of the guests became extremely seasick and his misery was intensified when, while he was hanging over the side, his dentures disappeared into the deep.

We decided to turn back and on the way, to cheer us all up, one of the anglers who had good sea-legs and had been trolling his line surreptitiously took out his own false teeth and cried, 'Look what I've brought up from the bottom.'

His toothless friend examined the dentures in hopeful anticipation then announced miserably, 'They are not mine' and threw them into the sea.

Not many years ago, I had the pleasure of fishing a certain beat on a little Scottish river where, in April, the salmon were stacked in the pools like sardines. A catch of more than 200 salmon by four rods in two weeks of that month was regular. There was only one drawback – the sewage effluent from a nearby town flowed into one of the best pools and, especially on a warm day, the stench, as well as the sight, could be unbearable.

The owner could have brought pressure to bear on the local authority but felt disinclined to do so. The only answer was to try to bring some pressure to bear on him.

One member of the April team was the then Lord Chancellor, the late Viscount Dilhorne, and his solemn advice, over brandy and cigars, was that one of the rods should be photographed fishing the offending pool in a gas mask and that news of that event should be leaked to the local newspaper. Naturally, the Lord Chancellor of England could not be photographed in such a circum-stance and the short straw was drawn by my husband, who donned a wartime gas mask, found locally, and fished away while being photographed.

The event was duly reported, commented upon and seen by the laird. Sadly, he did not turn his attention to

the local authority. He turned his rage on the anglers, who were sacked from the beat, Lord Chancellor and all. Like the laird, they were not amused.

The favourite recollection of **Michael Clark**, the former deputy chairman of Plessey, involves the owner of the other side of the river.

I was fishing Lady Bowden's water on the Test with my friend Christopher Thompson, opposite the glorious lawn that runs down the bank from the house then occupied by a fearsome old lady called Mrs Parker. She was sitting in state and suitably hatted under a great sunshade at the top of her lawn watching, with some distaste, us young men fishing from the opposite side.

A good fish was rising under her bank and with an almighty cast, which she could not fail to notice, I covered it, hooked it and, after much splashing, landed it. I should have resisted holding the trout up in the air and shaking it in triumph but, youth being what it is, I didn't. The old lady rose from her chair and like a great galleon taking on full sail came billowing down the lawn.

I had plenty of time to duck behind a convenient bush, leaving Christopher to address the next fish, which was rising steadily in midstream. He was so intent on his fishing that he had not seen the enemy descending and so was subjected to the full broadside of Mrs Parker's views on young men who covered her fish from Lady Bowden's bank.

Meanwhile I was in paroxysms behind my bush while Christopher, in spite of his protestations that he had not transgressed and had not even been fishing at the time, was ground down into apologising.

I was, myself, the victim of a riverside joke which I have not forgotten or been allowed to forget.

I was spinning the Ferry Stream on the Kinnaird beat of the Tay, from the bank, in moderately high water, while my husband was fishing the Junction pool, higher up, rowed by the delightful gillie John Lorimer, whom we shared.

I was quickly into a good salmon, which ran out a lot of line. To my horror, I saw the line part and disappear. My husband's remark to Lorimer that 'She's into a fish' had quickly been superseded by 'She must have been on the bottom' as he saw me tackling up again, out of earshot of my curses.

When we changed places I told them both that I had lost a big fish but doubted that either believed me. We had not been in the boat long when Lorimer remarked, 'I think Mr Chapman Pincher's into a fish.' We looked downstream and strange things were going on. My husband's rod was bent and he was walking back up the bank. He then ran to the water's edge, laid his rod down and began fiddling with it. 'I don't know what he's up to but it's not a fish,' Lorimer declared.

In fact, with almost his first cast, he had hooked my line with the fish still on it and, as he reeled it in, saw that the line was only very loosely attached to one of the treble hooks of his bait. He had immediately dropped the rod and rushed to knot the line securely to his bait. He then played the fish and landed it but we had lost interest and did not see that happen.

By the time I decided to go back to Kinnaird House, fishless, for tea my husband had disappeared down river. He joined the tea party about half an hour later and his first remark, loudly delivered, was 'How big do you say that fish was that you lost?'

'Over twenty pounds,' I replied in the full hearing of all our fishing pals.

'Well I can tell you it was only fifteen.'

'How could you possibly know that?'

'Because there's your bait,' he said, handing me my
2-inch brown-and-gold Devon with 20 yards of line neatly
coiled.

It was an unfair advantage to have taken but, I suppose,
as he said, 'irresistible'.

There are many occasions on the river when events
are not deliberately contrived but still produce some
memorable humour.

Like many an ardent fly fisher, a gentleman of my
acquaintance began his angling life as a bait fisher,
trotting maggots down the fast streams of northern England on very light tackle for anything he could tempt.
He also introduced his young wife to this quite difficult
art and, realising that the alternative was being left at
home, she tried her hand at it.

It was the custom, as it still may be, to have the maggots
in a linen bag slung from the neck so that, when wading,
they were handy when the hook needed to be rebaited
and a handful needed to be thrown into the water.

This pair were fishing away on the River Swale one
warm summer afternoon, with little luck, when a friend
came along the bank and suggested that they should all
try some miles higher up the river where he had special
permission.

They put their rods through the open car windows and
the lady climbed into the back while the husband rode
in the front with the driver. They had not gone far when
the lady, who had not taken the precaution of removing
her maggot bag from her neck, nodded off.

About half an hour later, as the car came to a stop,
she awoke and emitted a piercing scream. The fat
maggots – hundreds of them – had wriggled their way

106

out of the bag and into the interstices of her woollen jumper.

The lady's distress was only intensified as her husband took the only course of action – pulling the squirming garment over her head. It was more than wool which was being pulled over her eyes and many of the maggots inevitably fell into her long hair and elsewhere.

It said something for her character that, though the marriage eventually collapsed, this searing event was not the cause. Indeed, after the parting she remained a keen angler – mainly with maggots.

Lord Mason, the former Labour Defence Minister, who is now devoting much of his energy to angling affairs, provides a splendid example of unconscious humour from the waterside.

When fishing a lake known to contain large trout one is faced with a dilemma – whether to use a light-weight nylon cast, or leader as some call it, to ensure rising as many fish as possible, or to use heavy-duty nylon so that if a very large fish is hooked it will not be lost through breakage.

Very shortly after Sir Geoffrey Johnson-Smith, the very likeable Tory MP and former TV interviewer, had been knighted in 1982, he was fishing with me as a member of the Lords and Commons Fly Fishers. We were taking part in a match against a team of stage celebrities including, I believe, Frankie Vaughan and Bernard Cribbins. The venue was Bayham Abbey lake, on the Kent–Sussex border, which was well stocked with trout.

Honours were fairly even but looked like swinging our way when Geoffrey, who was fishing from the bank, hooked a very large trout and began to run with it. Sometimes this is necessary but Geoffrey was running

so far that we were constrained to shout and ask him why.

'I have no faith in my leader,' he cried. 'I don't trust my leader.'

These, of course, were cries guaranteed to make the headlines if literally interpreted. A high Tory running about in public shouting 'I have no faith in my leader,' so soon after Margaret Thatcher had recommended the Queen to confer a knighthood on him!

There and then we threatened to report him to the Second Lady but desisted when he was desolated by losing the fish, because his leader with a small 'l' had let him down.

Jason Garrett, proprietor of the London Lakes trout fishery in Tasmania, has also had one or two misunderstandings with the English language.

One does not have to meet many overseas visitors before realising that there are considerable differences in the ways English is used in the various countries where it is the native language.

Recently, I was describing the peculiarities of Tasmanian brown trout fishing to an American client, explaining that all our fish are completely wild and not artificially fed. One of their special characteristics is the way they 'tail' around the shores, exposing their tails above the water as they forage for food in the shallows.

'We stalk the shores for tails,' I explained. 'Sometimes, a tail will be motionless and can be spotted by the sun glistening on it.'

Back at the Lodge, his good lady inquired, 'How was it?'

'Oh fine, darling, just fine, but the guy's a little hard to understand. He spent most of the morning talking about tiles – bathroom tiles, I guess.'

On another occasion I was with a regular American visitor on a warm, breezy evening when one of the most productive methods is to put the fly out beyond the reeds and let it sit there until a trout spots it and rises to it. As it is necessary to connect quickly, I was telling him how an Australian lady angler had missed three good fish a couple of evenings previously by failing to strike fast enough. I had got to the stage of shouting to her 'Strike, STRIKE, for God's sake, STRIKE!', but to little avail.

On the way back the American, who was a most experienced angler, remarked, 'Strike! I must look up what it means in Webster's dictionary.'

Perhaps, again, it was the way I had pronounced it.

Usually, fishing is too solitary a sport to give rise to memorable repartee on the bankside but **Ernest Juer**, a Berkshire landowner and businessman, has sent me an example which has remained in his memory.

The Gredos mountains, north and west of Madrid, provide spectacular trout fishing and the official of the Parador de Turismo, who issued me with a day permit, suggested a briefing by the local doctor, whose clinic was to be found close to the river.

A dozen people seeking the doctor's healing aid must have held less attraction for him than I did when a message announcing my arrival reached him. I was waved in and begged his expertise.

The medic looked out of the window, sighed and said that conditions were difficult but within seconds he had opened the door to the waiting-room, cried that consultations were over and led me through the suffering throng to the riverbank. As we arrived, a Frenchman was packing up saying that the fishing was no good and the worst chance was in the pool I was about to try.

The good doctor fitted me up with a grey fly, instructed me to move several yards downstream and urged me to cast. He skilfully netted the resulting pound trout.

Eighty minutes and a dozen fish later, the French gentleman was so angry that he exclaimed, loudly in his own language, that God, for no good reason, always looks after the English.

'Not at all,' the doctor replied, in excellent French. 'Not the Lord, but his humble Spanish servant.'

———————◦————————

It must be rare for too many fish in a river to be a source of critical humour but **Dermot Wilson** has never forgotten such an occasion.

During the 1970s I spent a week fishing in Hampshire with one of America's foremost fishermen, Ernest Schweibert. He was politeness itself and a marvellous companion, but I could see that he was more than a little disconcerted to find just how heavily stocked most of the River Test is these days. Eventually, he expressed his disappointment: he had hardly expected the fabled Test to be so artificial or, at times, so easy.

I then took him, for interest, to one short stretch which I knew contained more stocked trout per square yard than any other. With considerable pride the keeper led him to a pool where he could see the serried ranks of huge rainbows lying side by side and looking for all the world like outsize sardines in an outsize tin.

'Good God!' exclaimed Ernest to the keeper, who was waiting for the usual compliment. 'How do you get them all in? With a Tokyo subway-pusher? Or with a shoehorn?'

111

Another incident involving a river where, though not artificially stocked, the trout have been so little fished that they are too easy has been drawn to my attention by my neighbour, **Major Anthony Stansfeld**, a senior Army helicopter pilot who is now in the commercial helicopter world.

The Falkland Islands are one of the world's most lovely remote areas. Still totally unspoiled, they have a remarkable initial similarity to the Outer Hebrides, only on a much larger scale. In 1982 I went there to run a large number of helicopters in the immediate aftermath of the war. Flying helicopters must be the best of all ways of seeing a country and it did not take long to work out which of the many rivers held the best potential for days off. The sea trout fishing was superb. All the larger rivers were filled with fish, many running to over ten pounds and some to over twenty. They derive from brown trout introduced into one easily accessible river by the settlers after the Second World War. They learned to go down to the sea to feed on the rich krill, which makes them grow rapidly, and have since spread to most of the big rivers on the islands. When they return to the rivers to spawn their appetite is voracious and their taste catholic. Any fly or spinner would normally bring a response on the first cast into a good pool. If there was no response after three casts it usually meant the pool was empty. It did not take long for the entire helicopter squadron's personnel to become heartily sick of endless fresh sea trout for dinner.

Soon after the end of the Falklands war, the high-priced visitors started arriving on the islands – assorted MPs from all parties, high-ranking officers from all services and senior civil servants. Also several journalists. For all their beauty, the Falkland Islands cannot be said to be the best place for entertaining visitors, unless they are keen naturalists. However, some of them were fishermen and this gave the commander an easy option. I would be summoned and told to take them fishing. Luckily the general was a great fisherman himself so this was no ordeal for either of us. We would take the visitor to wherever was on the programme for the day, and on the way back drop off at some remote and probably unfished pool. It was always a success. However incompetent the visitor, it could always be arranged for him to catch something, even if it meant somebody else hooking the fish.

Many a visitor was sent home to the United Kingdom with a bundle of sea trout and a feeling that, whatever the press was saying, the Falkland Islands were a marvellous place.

The general was a most affable gentleman. He got on with everyone and could carry on long and amusing conversations from the back seat of the helicopter while I flew with the VIP sitting in the co-pilot's seat. However, the minister defeated him. He was a really senior politician who had had more than a little to do with the war and his memories may not have been too happy. He remained virtually monosyllabic the entire time. Whether this was a reflection of the terror he felt as a result of my flying I am not sure.

As it was impossible to get round the Falklands without using a helicopter, the minister spent rather a long time over five days in the general's company and mine. Our cheery conversation soon started to become stilted in the face of terse negatives, affirmatives and grunts. The general did his best but even he eventually relapsed into unusual silence. I carried on in my best tour-guide manner, pointing out battlefields, penguin colonies, seals, and so forth. Still little interest. I hardly dared bring up the frivolous subject of fishing. However, it was difficult to refrain from pointing out some of the better pools as we sped over them. No response. With only one more day to go I had rather run out of small talk and the general had given up. Suddenly and after several minutes' silence between Goose Green and Stanley, the great man gave tongue. 'Any chance of doing some fishing?'

Now senior ministers are not supposed to have spare time, every moment being carefully programmed. However, this was not an opportunity to be missed. 'I'm sure there is some time available tomorrow afternoon before the minister leaves,' I remarked casually as we swept into land. 'Right! Organise it,' the general responded.

Well, of course, there wasn't any time. Next morning was totally full and there was a heavy lunch with the Royal Engineers before the minister was due back in Stanley for the long and uncomfortable flight home in a Hercules transport. There was a small gap in the programme if lunch did not take too long and there were two excellent pools on the route just itching to be fished.

Next morning I packed three telescopic spinning rods in the helicopter boot and we set off. Lunch started late and the Engineers had every intention of making sure that the minister was well fed and watered. I could see it going on until at least three o'clock. Port and brandy had appeared in the background and the engineers were getting well dug in. I could see the general beginning to squirm and the minister surreptitiously looking at his watch. The fishing trip was looking decidedly gloomy. In my lowly place at the end of the table there was little I could do. In desperation I wrote a note to the Engineer colonel, which was passed up the table – 'The minister, the general and I all want to go fishing. If we don't leave now it's too late.'

I could see the colonel weighing his career prospects. Port and brandy disappeared, excuses were made and we were off.

The pool was about a hundred yards long. The minister took the bottom, the general the top and I fitted in the middle. In the next forty minutes the minister, who was a competent fisherman, was into fish continuously and landed some six sea trout while the general, who had

114

three, was tactless enough to catch the biggest, a fish of about six pounds. After forty minutes the fishing slowed and the general suggested a change of pool. By now the time was critical. The plane was leaving in an hour and we were about forty miles from Stanley airport. However, the general had the bit between his teeth as he remarked, 'Even the bloody RAF can't leave without the minister.'

The next pool was again about a hundred yards long and the minister cast into the tail. After five casts there was no sign of a take so I suggested that if he ran to the top of the pool there would be just time for a few casts. The heather-like scrub along the pool made running difficult but the minister managed it. He arrived at the head of the pool gasping and just managed to cast between titanic breaths. The spinner had only just hit the water when it was taken by a large fish. The minister played it well and landed a magnificent sea trout, just larger than the general's. We leapt back into the helicopter and flew flat out to the airport. The fish were all put into sacks and we landed behind the Hercules, which had already taxied out on to the runway. A worried civil servant carried out the heavy sack into the aircraft and it was off.

The minister's visit had ended on a good note and the general subsequently received a well deserved knight-hood. I would like to think that the minister's last fish helped a little.

———————◦◦◦———————

The young man in the following story, contributed by **Jan Eckman**, Vice Chairman of the Svenska Handelsbanken of Stockholm, was not so lucky in earning the approval of a higher authority.

General Franco, whom I did not admire, was a keen salmon fisherman and tried his luck in the rivers of northern Spain each spring. To guarantee him maximum luck – he was bad-tempered and resentful as he grew older – an army unit was stationed along the river for his personal protection but also to guard his favourite pools against poachers and report on the run of salmon in them. When a particular pool reached its maximum capacity for fish it was closed off with wire netting at both ends.

The Caudillo always invited a number of important people as spectators and major appointments, especially among the military, were often announced on the river-bank. It was said that the better the fishing, the more generals were appointed. As soon as he hooked and played a fish he would summon one of the VIP spectators to gaff it and it was generally believed that, if the gaffing was expertly accomplished, the lucky man could look forward to promotion. I did not witness the occasion of which I write, and relate it as it was told to me.

One year, on the first fishing morning, the man chosen for the first salmon was a young major and sighs of surprise and envy came from the rest. Having been warned of his leader's fishing habits in advance, he had taken the precaution of practising with a gaff, allegedly from the fencing master of his regiment, and had been seen running up and down a river gaffing out bags filled with wood shavings. His nerves well under control, he ran swiftly to the water's edge and stood prepared, with his gaff, in the right position.

After a few minutes he saw a large salmon gliding towards him, gently slid the gaff into the water and, with the panache of a matador, swung the fish towards the dictator, who smiled a contented smile.

The envious watchers just had time to whisper that the major's promotion was assured when Franco's rod was torn out of his unsuspecting hands and disappeared into the pool. The terrible truth was obvious to all – there were so many salmon in the pool that the major had gaffed the wrong one!

116

David Clarke, Vice-President of the Atlantic Salmon Trust, considers an inflated idea.

The Atlantic Salmon Trust holds annual postal auctions of various fishings and the Tulchan Estate very kindly donated a week for five rods on the Spey. This was successfully bid for by the chairman of the Dangerous Sports Society. He was so pleased that he rang up and suggested that he would like to give the Trust some publicity. He explained that he happened to have a thirty-foot tall inflatable kangaroo and he proposed to float down the Spey sitting in its pouch, fishing as he went. He also suggested that a friend, who had a fifteen foot high pink elephant should follow him down.

In the end, we persuaded him that such publicity might be counter-productive, as it certainly would have been to the fishing, and perhaps this was fortunate because, not long afterwards, it was reported in a reliable newspaper that the captain of a Boeing jumbo jet had needed to take evasive action when he had encountered a thirty-foot high kangaroo at 10,000 feet on his flight from Heathrow to Paris. There was a picture of the kangaroo supported by three large balloons and there, sure enough, was the chairman of the Dangerous Sports Society sitting in its pouch and grinning from ear to ear.

Sometimes it is the fish that plays the joke, as **Dermot Wilson** found when trying to educate a friend.

There was a time in my tender youth, some two hundred years or so ago, when I must, surely, have been the most devoted disciple that Skues ever had. Skues was, in all ways, my fishing guru. So when Ian, a Scottish friend of my own age, came to fish our southern chalk streams for the first time I naturally knew how to set him on the true path to success and righteousness.

'We shan't do very well until we've caught one trout and marrow-scooped him,' I told him, condescendingly, when we started out on the Itchen. 'Then we'll know just what all the trout are feeding on. You may not bother about it in Sutherland but I assure you that it is essential down here.'

Somewhat to my chagrin, it was Ian who caught the first fish and I was soon at work on it with a genuine silver Georgian marrow-scoop and a white enamel bowl – *à la* Skues. When the prescribed ritual had been completed we both peered excitedly into the bowl to see the contents of the stomach. There it lay in all its solitary glory – one large red rubber band!

'I'm afraid I don't have one of those in my fly box,' Ian remarked as he went off and caught three brace of good trout. I caught one – trout, not brace.

———————————⊃●⊂———————————

The extraordinary way in which a small grayling successfully fooled an American Angler is described by **Colonel I. H. McCausland.**

Richard Banbury, a qualified casting instructor and the manager of the Orvis tackle shop in Stockbridge, where I live, took a good American fisherman to Orvis's Broadlands beat, which used to be part of the salmon fishing there. As is common on the lower stretches of the River Test, there is a series of wooden groynes to increase the flow of the water.

The American hooked a good brown trout of about four pounds which zipped all over the place. After quite a battle the line and leader caught in the woodwork of one of the groynes and the fish escaped. No sooner had this happened than a six-inch grayling took the fly, freeing the leader and the line in the process. The grayling was duly landed and it had all happened so quickly that the

fisherman was totally unaware of the switch and thought that it was the fish he had originally hooked. On seeing a grayling for the first time he was full of praise for its fighting ability!

Until my husband retired from Fleet Street we lived in a lovely sixteenth-century farmhouse in Surrey. In the garden, which was surrounded by farmland, there was the old farm pond which we had stocked with golden orfe and tench. There were several types of ornamental ducks and wild mallard flighted in at night. We knew of the existence of a couple of small carp – about three pounds in weight – which must have been put in the pond by a previous owner and often wondered whether there was anything bigger lurking among the water-lilies but never saw anything. That is, until a certain practical joker, called Jimmy James, heard of our curiosity.

One day, while my husband was at the office, Jimmy called at the house and asked if I would keep a secret. He took me to his car and there in the boot, in a tank of water, was the biggest carp I had ever seen – all of ten pounds. He was a fisherman but had not caught the carp. He had taken the trouble to buy it from a man who owned a brickyard pond and had netted the fish out specially to order. He slipped the fish into our pond and I promised to say nothing about it to anyone.

The joke appeared to have fallen flat until one evening when my husband was feeding the golden orfe with bread. A duck was swimming towards a piece of bread when Jimmy's carp suddenly surfaced underneath it like a submarine and tipped it over. My husband couldn't believe his eyes and rushed into the house crying, 'There's the most enormous carp in the pond. It's just upskittled one of the ducks. I always told you there could be a monster there! It's amazing how they can hide themselves.'

I pretended to be amazed and raced out to see the monster, which by that time had disappeared.

'Are you sure you weren't seeing things?' I asked.

'No! I tell you it's all of ten pounds. It could even be bigger.'

I said nothing until I saw Jimmy some time later and told him what had happened. He laughed as heartily as if he had been there to see the event.

'I caught him that time. What a coup! What a coup! Don't tell him!'

I thought it odd that anyone could go to such trouble and expense to set up a joke he was most unlikely to witness. But then, men are odd. Especially fishermen.

INTRUDERS

Fisherwomen have their oddities too, as **Dermot Wilson** discovered, rather disconcertingly.

Waterside wooing is no good. Any woman who is sensible enough to go fishing will be far too astute to allow her endeavours to be interrupted by anything so trivial as romance. I learned this lesson many years ago when I was frantically, desperately, in love with a girl whose father owned a stretch of a famous Scottish salmon river. (Whether this asset had anything to do with my feelings towards her I honestly can't remember.)

I fondly imagined that I was getting along with her famously, especially when she invited me to stay with her father and fish his water. On the first morning we were by the riverside early. It was a bitterly cold March day and her father's instructions were that we could only fish one rod between us and that we should spin. Like the perfect gentlemen I was trying to emulate, I insisted that my loved one should begin while I sat on the bank keeping warm with a bottle of cherry brandy. I regarded this as most unselfish.

For the next hour I watched my love spinning, which she did impeccably and with great patience. At frequent intervals I called out such words of encouragement and endearment as occurred to me. She never so much as saw a salmon and stamped up the bank saying, 'Now you take this useless rod and give me a cherry brandy.'

Being hers to command, I picked up the rod and flung the minnow somewhere into the river. A terrible thing happened. On that very first random chuck I hooked and eventually landed a 17-pound salmon. And was the apple of my eye pleased with me? Did she congratulate me with warmth and affection? No. She hardly ever spoke to me again.

125

The writer, **David Barr**, also had good occasion to deplore the intrusion of romance.

July is not a great month on the Aberdeenshire Dee but, this time, we had been blessed with a 3-foot flood. Fish were moving all over the Upper Blackhall beat, which we had taken for a week. Before I went to the top pool, called the Morrell, the gillie, Ian Anderson, warned me, 'There are places where you might need a tailer or an active friend.' Wise Ian!

My friend and co-rod, James, was fishing a little lower down; he was also squandering his time celebrating a wedding anniversary with his wife. Never mix anything, I tend to say, with salmon fishing.

I told him that I would be fishing the tail of the pool above him and suggested, in case of emergency, that he should join me in ten minutes or so. Normally he was as reliable as the turning of the tide.

As I reached the tail of the pool a fish showed and, from the bank, I cast over it. There was a boil; the line tightened and an early leap revealed that I had hooked something only a little smaller than a shark. Fifteen minutes passed before I began to gain control. Another five and a massive salmon, brass-coloured in the stained water, swam by me. 'James!' I yelled repeatedly, but answer came there none.

Five minutes more and there it was, more or less dormant in front of me. Nosing it into some reeds, and still yelling 'James!', I slid down the six-foot bank wondering how, in the name of Izaak Walton, I would ever lift it out and up. Shaking with awe, I carefully gripped its tail only to find that it was too monstrous to get my fingers round. It would have been as easy to grasp a passing oak trunk.

The pressure roused the fish, which took off on a hundred-yard tour, but not many minutes later it was back in the same position. By then I was hoarse from shouting. Gently I turned its head to try something I had never tried before – sticking my fingers into its gills. I was on the verge of my big effort when the fish, sensing what was in store, shook its head and the hook slipped quietly out.

Dazed and sick with disappointment I threw down my rod and ran downstream. There, in the bracken a hundred yards below, were James and his wife, murmuring sweet nothings. It was quite an hour before I could bring myself to speak to him.

———————>o<———————

I know from my own experience that the lady in question should have been highly flattered by being given higher priority than the fishing. On the first occasion I accompanied my husband-to-be on a fishing trip he spent most of the first evening tying up golden sprats when he could have been attending to me. Nevertheless, one should never underestimate the power of a woman. The next story which might well be entitled 'Putting the boot in', has been kindly contributed by Admiral of the Fleet Sir Henry Leach.

Rear-Admiral George Thring and his wife, Bette (a skilled wielder of the salmon rod), were up for the grouse on a moor at Gledfield, by Bonar Bridge in Sutherland. It had been a long, hot summer, perhaps the driest in living memory. Most of the burns were dried out; only the deeper pools held a few inches of water and these were evaporating fast. Still, the birds were strong and plentiful and, though it might be hopeless for fishermen, shooting prospects were good.

Bette was not shooting but was helping to pick up. She was wearing gumboots to protect her legs from the heather.

When the party assembled for the picnic lunch, Bette was missing but she couldn't be far away and by the time the Guns were enjoying their second drink she appeared. 'Quite a productive last drive!' she announced, holding up a seven-pound salmon.

The party was dumbfounded. It was hot and they had imbibed, but a salmon in a grouse drive far from any river.

'I was crossing a little burn,' Bette explained. 'It was practically dry and I heard a splash. When I investigated, there, in a tiny hollow in a rock with just enough water to cover it, was this salmon. It was obviously going to die so I took off one of my gumboots and used it as a landing net by pushing the fish in. I looked for a bigger pool to put it in but there wasn't one. What else could I do but put it out of its misery?'

What else indeed!

It is well established that women have a penchant for catching big salmon – like the all-time British record of 64 pounds caught on the Tay and the English record of 59 ½ pounds on the Wye. Relatively recently, I had the pleasure of meeting an old lady who had caught one of these exceptional salmon on the Tay. She was visiting Kinnaird House and recalled how, at the age of seventeen, she had been sent out to fish along with the other guests and, on returning to lunch, saw a fish of well over forty pounds laid out on the front steps. It had been caught by the laird, her uncle I believe, and he was very proud of it until she produced the 50-pounder she had just landed. It resides to this day on the billiard-room wall and is the biggest fish ever to have been caught there.

Though happy for the young girl, the laird was not best pleased. Men do not like their angling aces trumped. They are usually more experienced and more expert fishers than we are but, perhaps, we are just more fortunate, or maybe more patient. I always take longer to fish a pool than my husband does and it often pays off.

Whatever the reason, it needs to be watched in the interests of marital bliss. Whenever I catch a salmon I pray that my husband will have one when he comes in.

On my first morning fishing in Iceland I was taken to a pool called the Aquarium and by lunch time had five salmon. Fortunately my husband had four from a pool called Broken Bank, taken on four consecutive casts. I ended the day with nine to my husband's seven – not too flagrant a difference but, perhaps, not to be repeated too often. Happily, by the end of our eight days he had fifty-three to my thirty-eight, which was just right. Honour was saved all round. After all, it is Man that is supposed to be the hunter!

<hr />

At least my husband is happy to have me with him by the waterside. My friend **Anthony Prendergast**, the former Lord Mayor of Westminster, whose wife does not fish, was more than disconcerted by the female company he encountered recently.

In the summer of 1986 I went to fish in the north-west of Scotland, staying at a hotel at Lochinver which has salmon water on the River Kirkaig. It is a short but very pretty river, rushing through little gorges and terminating at some falls below a loch. The only problem there is that in summer there are hordes of midges and they are very ferocious.

I had been up the middle beat on my first day, which the midges ruined for me, swarming all over my hands and face the whole time. I had no veil, which anglers there normally wear, and the local fishing-tackle shop could not supply one, so I decided to improvise.

I bought myself a pair of ladies' tights in the village store, cut off one leg and impregnated it with fly repellent. Next morning, on arrival at the lower beat which had been allocated to me, I put on my mask and dispensed with a hat. I knew what I looked like – a bank robber – having tried it on in front of the mirror back at the hotel, but I did not expect to see anyone else.

I fished steadily throughout the morning and concentrated on the Old Bridge pool, where I saw fish moving. I had been down it twice with a Green Highlander and

came out to change my fly. As I turned a small corner, looking for a flat place to sit, I spotted a mother and her two daughter having a picnic. The lady looked up, screamed 'A rapist!' at the top of her voice and took off with her children, shouting warnings to other people on the way.

Slinking back to the river, I pulled off the stocking mask and decided I had better change to a Blue Charm and put up with the midges.

———————————⊃●⊂———————————

Tony should have realised before donning that stocking mask that there is a golden rule of the countryside which one ignores at one's peril – however isolated you think you are there may be others lurking about.

As all female anglers know, river banks present a more difficult problem than they do for men when nature's calls clamour for answer, especially when chest waders are being worn. One lady, who was fishing the Spey, felt particularly secure in this circumstance because she had taken a beat with both banks and the gillies were known to her to be at lunch. Totally alone, she selected a spot by a sharp bend of the river shielded from the roadway by a belt of conifers. Nothing could look safer as she lowered her waders and all else. Sadly, a few seconds later ten canoeists glided by and they did not spare the lady their cheers and tally-hos.

———————————⊃●⊂———————————

Sometimes the person watching may have evil intent, or, at least, appear to have, as **Joan Hirsch** recalls with respect to her late soldier-husband, a widely loved and respected sportsman.

131

In the difficult and dangerous period immediately following the creation of the Irish Free State, my late husband, Jack, who was a very English army officer and had previously served in Ireland during the troubles, decided to take a chance. So great was his love of salmon fishing that he went to his father's estate at Ballyhooly to fish that beat of the Blackwater river for several days.

He believed himself to be entirely on his own on the water but had not been fishing very long when he sensed another presence. He looked around and saw a disembodied bowler hat, of the type then called a billycock, bobbing about in the little copse behind the pool. Understandably, his immediate thought was that some vengeful Irishman was lining him up to take a pot-shot at him but, with some trepidation, he fished bravely on.

Having finished the pool and risen nothing, he felt that discretion could now be shown. He reeled up and started his fifteen-minute brisk walk back to the house. All the time he was aware of the billycock hat bouncing along from bush to bush behind him. He resisted the urge to run for it and eventually made the house with some relief.

That evening an Irish countryman, wearing a billycock hat, as was the common practice, called to see him. He expressed his delight at seeing the Major back and trusted that he would enjoy some good fishing. In the broadest brogue he told him:

'Rest assured, Major, that it is Oi meself who will be kapin' an eye on ye for the remainder of yer visit. In fact, this very afthernoon Oi was watchin' over ye, though you never spotted me at arl – which was just what Oi'd intended.'

———————◦———————

Of all sports, fishing, the essence of tranquillity, is the least likely to be associated with armed strife. **Lord Sieff**, the President of Marks & Spencer, who loves trout

fishing, recalls an exception to this generalisation.

During a business visit to Israel in the mid-1960s I thought it would be pleasant to take a little time off and do some trout fishing, having heard that some rivers had been stocked. I therefore consulted the top man in the fish world there, the delightful General Abraham Yoffee, who had worked wonders in creating nature reserves while at the same time making malarial swamps available for agriculture.

The General told me that the best river was on the northeast border but warned, 'If you cast more than halfway across the river you will be fishing in Syrian water and you might get shot.' Needless to say, I did not bother to go.

Shortly after the famous victories of the Six Day War, when I was in Israel again, I happened to meet General Yoffee. 'By the way,' he said, laconically, 'if you want to go and fish that river you can cast right across it now.'

———————————⊃●⊂———————————

When fishing the Spey from a boat, Lady Sopwith used to have her shotgun with her in case any passing goosanders or mergansers, which prey on salmon fry, came within range. While gunfire does not usually mix well with the peace of a river, sporting manager **Tony Ingram** once had to contend with it, among other inconveniences.

As you journey the Jasper National Park in Canada, there is one thing you notice above all else – the 'Danger: Grizzly Bear' signs. Various precautions were recommended in the event of meeting one, such as ringing a bell, climbing the nearest tree or lying down and feigning death. At least the Indians seemed friendly as my brother Mike and I arrived at the Buras Lake area to pick up some fishing tackle before our attempt on the coho salmon and steelheads in the Kispiox river.

The beautiful Kispiox flows in the bottom of a wooded ravine and, after camping overnight, we decided that Mike would fish upstream towards Wolf Creek while I would work downstream to Bear Caves.

Plenty of fish were moving as I approached the tail of a very likely pool. Soon I thought I heard heavy footsteps above the roar of the water and stopped fishing to listen. They became louder and nearer with the cracking and breaking of branches. I froze, sure that a grizzly was on its way down to fish for her cubs. I had not seen a grizzly but I had stood in the footprints of one making my own size twelves look small. If fully grown, the 1 ½-ton beast was likely to be 12 feet tall on her hind legs!

As the nearest tree was fifty yards away and I was not prepared to lie in the water feigning death and I had no bell, I began singing 'Land of Hope and Glory' at the top of my voice in the hope of scaring the beast away. But the noises came nearer. I could hear it as it splashed into the water into which I waded up to my waist, hoping that it would be more interested in the fish than in me.

During those truly terrifying moments I had not realised that my spinner was still trailing downstream and suddenly my rod was almost pulled out of my hand by what seemed like a large coho salmon. That was the first, and last, moment in my life when I did not care if the fish got off, however big it might be.

Suddenly there was an almighty bang followed by another and several grunting noises. Happily the grunts sounded human and the bangs were definitely gunshots. My fish was still on as I was confronted by a very fat Indian squaw with a baby strapped to her back. Farther downstream an Indian brave, whom I assumed to be her husband, stood, rifle at shoulder, blazing away at an old tree stump on the other side of the river.

The fish was still on and doing what it liked as the squaw laughed and lifted her skirts above her waist. She then produced a small telescopic rod from what passed for her knickers, put a bait on the line and hurled it into midstream. Immediately she had a salmon on, which she pulled in unceremoniously, refusing an offer of my landing net. Over a space of about ten minutes she killed four salmon while the brave pumped scores of rounds into the fast-disintegrating tree stump.

The squaw then packed her rod back in her underwear, gave the baby a slice of raw fish, grunted to her husband and departed into the trees. He raised his hand, twirling his rifle in the other, and vanished with her.

My fish was still on but I could not bring it to the net. When I did it turned out to be only a twelve-pounder foul-hooked in the tail.

'You look pale,' my brother observed when he eventually appeared. After an experience like that I felt that I had good reason to be.

My neighbour **Anthony Stansfeld** has described an incident in which real warfare, or its consequences, intruded into the riverside peace.

In the immediate aftermath of the Falklands war, I was flying a helicopter back to Port Stanley, where we had to land to look at a building which had been used by the Argentinians. Close by was a most attractive sea-trout pool on a large river called the San Carlos. I had with me a telescopic spinning rod already equipped with a Mepps spoon and took the opportunity to see if there were any fish.

Every cast brought an immediate response and, working my way up the pool, I caught several sea trout up to seven pounds and some kelts, which I returned. Half-way up the pool, beside a peat hag, I noticed a large and obviously Argentinian rucksack, which must have been discarded by some soldier trying to retreat back to Stanley. Clearly visible in it were binoculars and a special night-viewing system.

These were too good to leave behind, but equally obvious underneath the rucksack were several hand grenades. Whether they had been abandoned in the haste to cross the river to evade the pursuing SAS patrols or whether it was a deliberate booby trap was difficult to determine. It seemed risky to leave the bag in such an obvious fishing spot or where some shepherd might pay dearly for his curiosity. The professional bomb disposers were heavily overworked, so precision casting was brought into play.

After several attempts, a Mepps spoon was landed on the rucksack and I retired to cover, paying out line as I went. Once safely behind a peat hag I pulled the line several times and, as nothing happened, it seemed safe to look at the grenades, which still had their pins in.

I liberated the loot, as spoils for the unit, and disposed of the grenades.

———————◦———————

A devastating experience resulting from the assumption that nobody else was about by the riverside befell one of the American Senators for Wyoming, **Malcolm Wallop**.

Before the days when I became involved in politics, I was fishing Little Goose Creek in the Big Horn Mountains, in my home state of Wyoming, along with two friends. The Creek, which runs through a canyon, has perpetually provided wonderful trout fishing for those happy to catch fish up to two pounds on light fly tackle in fast water. So far as we knew, we had the river to ourselves and by lunch time we had all either secured our limit of ten or caught enough to satisfy our appetite for sport.

After a sandwich lunch by the stream, and in the exuberance of youth, we decided to climb up the canyon to see

137

the view. Near the top we encountered a huge boulder, weighing at least two tons and so precariously placed that it would obviously not be long before further erosion of the soil sent it crashing down into the water below. Having nothing better to do, we decided to help it on its way and with a little digging and much pushing we succeeded.

The boulder did all we expected of it. Crashing down the canyon side it hit another rock and bounced high in the air, eventually landing in the river far below with a colossal splash.

Pleased with our effort, we made our way back to the bottom and were astonished to find another fisherman there. He made no mention of the boulder but simply asked if we had seen his friend, who, he believed, had been fishing in that part of the river. We looked at each other in deep dismay and went off to look for the missing angler. There was no sign of him and the same thought occurred to all three of us – he was dead under the boulder.

By the time we had moved out of the canyon we were all quite terrified and fell to wondering which form of homicide we would be charged with and how we would defend ourselves. We knew that we would have to report our folly if the man was missing so we simply sat and waited at a spot where the angler we had met would eventually have to emerge.

It was some hours later when a car came out of the canyon. To our intense relief and joy it contained two men.

I have never forgotten the experience and what might have happened just because we caught too many trout too quickly.

———————⟶•⟵———————

When you are fishing away contentedly, with little though for anybody or anything else, there may even be a water bailiff or licence inspector tucked away watching you. **Lord Mason**'s experience was all the more piquant because he is Chairman of the Anglers Co-operative Association, a member of the Salmon and Trout Association National Council and a member of the National Rivers Authority Advisory Committee.

The Houses of Lords and Commons have a Fly Fishing club which pits its wits against Lloyds lawyers in an annual competition on a stillwater trout lake in the south of England. It was an evening match – from 6 to 9 p.m. – and I arrived at the fishing lodge before 6 to inquire about licences. I was told that none were available.

As we had booked the water and nobody else would be fishing and we had all been prepared to buy licences we decided to go ahead and fish.

We were nicely into our sport, at about 7.30, when a water authority licence inspector suddenly appeared and asked six Members of Parliament – three lords and three commoners – and six distinguished lawyers for their licences. Only one licence was forthcoming – from one of the commoners. The inspector meant business. Names and addressed were taken and all the offenders eventually received notice to provide written explanations and to stand by for summonses.

After weeks of anxious waiting we were let off. But just imagine what a court appearance by the defendants would have done for the newspapers. What a field day the gossip columnists would have enjoyed!

The question which has since niggled me is, who had tipped off the inspector? I do not think that he was there by chance. I think we can rule out the commoner who had the licence. I incline to the belief that it was some irate local angler who had been denied his evening's fishing. Anyway, we shall never get caught that way again.

On several occasions I have been surprised to find that I was not alone on a river. On one of them I was fishing the famous Roe Pot pool on the Dee from the Inchmarlo side, totally engrossed in casting my fly at a nice salmon which was showing consistently. It is a beautiful pool; nobody was fishing the other side and I was very happy to be alone.

Hearing a sound, I turned to see a stranger carrying a pack on his back and holding a radio aerial.

'I hope you don't catch that fish,' he remarked affably.

'Why?'

'Because that's Fred. I've been following Fred for weeks and want to go on following him.'

He then explained that he was a fishery researcher and that Fred had been netted much lower down the river and had been fitted with a miniature radio transmitter in the form of a capsule inserted down its mouth and into its stomach. As, salmon do not feed in fresh water, the obstruction in the stomach was of no consequence and did not, apparently, incommode the fish. Certainly Fred seemed to be behaving normally, in that he couldn't care less about my fly.

While I continued to cast for Fred, wondering whether, in the circumstances, I would have to put him back if I caught him, the scientist explained that he had several other 'radio-active' fish transmitting in different ways so that they could all be identified when tracked down. One particularly surprising discovery had been made — Fred and his like do not always progress upstream as was formerly believed. Sometimes they go downstream again for several miles before turning round and swimming up again. This seems to be a waste of energy but the scientist explained that the fish are looking for the tributary or stretch in which they were hatched, and sometimes they miss it and go back down in search of it.

A mile or so below the Roe Pot there is a tributary, called the Feugh, which joins the Dee opposite the Banchory Lodge Hotel. From my bedroom window there I could sit and watch the salmon and grilse showing at the mouth of the Feugh before going up or going on. I wondered whether Fred was one of them, having changed his mind after my encounter with him. Anyway, I'm glad I didn't catch him. If he had been my first fish that day I still do not know whether I would have put him back or kept him. Perhaps it would have depended on whether the tracker had still been watching me.

Fred was to be detected, a few weeks later, higher up the river by a more exalted tracker – the Queen Mother. Her Majesty was on the Balmoral beat and, when the researcher appeared, was so intrigued that she insisted on donning the back-pack and taking the aerial. After a long walk along the bank she tracked down two tagged salmon, one of which was Fred.

It had been hoped that Fred would make it back to the sea to be detected again, in a later season, on a return journey up his native river. Sadly, however, he died after spawning and the last bleep from him was as a dead kelt.

I never thought that I would hear my husband say that he was sorry to have caught a salmon but that happened one winter's day on the Upper Blackhall beat of the Dee. He had hooked and landed a 14-pound springer and noticed a tag on its adipose fin stating that it had been tagged in Greenland and giving the date and address to which the tag should be returned. While not normally given to such penitent thoughts, he told the gillie that it seemed a shame to kill the fish when it had battled its way so far, against so many hazards.

'You had better give up fishing, sir, if you think that way,' the gillie said as he dispatched the salmon.

———————⊷⊶———————

My husband will never give up fishing. It will have to give him up and the same applies to **Lord Sieff**, who also had regrets, though apparently only once, as he testifies.

On a beat on the upper reaches of the River Test which I rented for several years there was a large brown trout easily recognisable because, for some reason, it was strongly striped across its back. Its regular lie was in a bay on the far side of a narrow part of the stream. Once I had spotted it I tried for it, conscientiously, but every time I managed to make a reasonable cast the fish swam up to inspect my fly, turned away and then, within a few seconds, took a natural fly. I was well used to this behaviour, but with this fish it never varied in the many times I fished for it in my first season on the river.

The following year the trout, now larger and more strongly marked, was still lying in its little bay and the previous year's performance was repeated throughout the second season.

I tried for it again and again in the third year, by which time it was a fine fish, and halfway through the season it made the fatal mistake and, to my astonishment, rose ferociously and took the fly. As I played it I began to feel pangs of remorse and was determined to release it. Sadly it had taken the fly so savagely and so deep that I could not remove it without first dispatching the fish.

I have never killed a trout with greater regret. I felt that I had murdered an old friend who had given me the thrill of anticipation for three years and was reminded of my deed every time I passed the bay.

One can usually put such a fish back safely, after holding it gently, head upstream, until it has regained its strength. But they are not always grateful.

Casting into a small pond a few yards from the River Kennet, having seen a commotion in the water, my husband hooked and landed a huge brown trout. The pond had been a stew some years previously and there were one or two large fish in it. As the pond was very near the fishing hut, my husband took the fish over to the river, left it there in his net, and brought the weighing scales to the fish. It was over seven pounds and was the biggest brownie he had ever caught.

At that moment the sun came out and the cock fish looked so beautiful that my husband decided to release it into the river, where someone might catch it later in circumstances more worthy of such a splendid creature. He held the fish gently in the water until it was sufficiently recovered and as he released it the trout turned, quite deliberately, and bit him severely on the thumb, drawing a lot of blood.

Such ingratitude has no doubt happened before, but the experience described by **Veronica Weld-Blundell** is probably unique.

Some years ago I went down to one of our pools on the River Hodder in north Lancashire to fish in what appeared to be impossible conditions. The river was in full spate after several days of rain and the only likely bait was a big Toby. During the night a very large branch of a tree had been swept down the river and had become embedded in the sandbank on which I stood to try my luck. After less than ten minutes I was into a good fish. I had almost managed to beach it when off it went in a last rush – straight into the branch. In the end I had to break the line and return home very despondent.

The next day was beautiful and the river had dropped dramatically so I returned to try my luck with the fly. After a couple of casts I noticed what appeared to be a large salmon floating on its side round and round in the large pool. The fish seemed to be dead and I though it might be the one I had lost on the previous day.

I put down my rod and waded into the tail end of the stream to try to grab it by the gills as it came round. As I stood with my hands poised in the water, the fish suddenly sprang to life and, from a distance of a couple of yards, came at me like an arrow and seized my thumb in its jaws. I threw myself upon it and while getting my fingers of the other hand into its gills we had a very wet tussle. I managed to get the fish out on to the bank with my thumb still firmly gripped in its mouth.

The fish — an 18-pound cock, and not the one I had lost — had pierced right through the thumb-nail and I needed medical treatment.

What had been responsible for the salmon's extraordinary behaviour, which was more like that of a shark? I consulted an expert fisherman, who took the view that the fish had been hooked and lost after an exhausting fight further upstream and was floating about while recovering. Then, suddenly seeing my fingers, it had mistaken them for prawns and had struck in a moment of aggression.

Whatever the explanation, I had been definitely and firmly caught by that salmon, though I exacted my revenge. It smoked very well.

———————————⇒●⊂———————————

The revenge which a fish can exact may be of a delayed-action nature, as **Ernest Juer** experienced in a most extra-ordinary way.

In the 1960s, when I was in East Africa for lengthy periods, I would hire a self-drive light aircraft and fly to a camp on the shore of Lake Rudolf, now called Lake Turkana, in northern Kenya. There in the greenish waters of this long lake, which has been called the Jade Sea, I would fish from the bank for the fierce and ferocious tigerfish and from a boat for Nile perch, which commonly reached 250 pounds in weight.

It was an exciting and yet relaxing place. The desert air was dry, clean and filled with music at night. There was the sound of camel bells as the nomadic Turkana tribe's herds went by in hundreds. Hippos — since extinguished — crocodiles and flamingoes lined the shores. A hot spring provided a natural bath. And the fishing was terrific.

The tigerfish were so keen to hook themselves that when one was fought to the bank and placed back in the water with a Mepps spoon dangling near, it would seize the bait again as soon as it had recovered sufficient strength. On several occasions I had catches of Nile perch in excess of 1,500 pounds and, as the firm, white flesh of these fish makes excellent eating, I could make most of my expenses by selling great fillets of them in Nairobi or Kampala. I liked eating them myself but, for some reason, became so allergic to them that they made my ankles swell to an enormous size.

Some twelve years after my last visit to Lake Rudolf my wife and I were in Tehran and, bored with the procrastinations of doing business there, we decided to get out quickly. The only available plane was the El Al flight to Tel Aviv and it was so hot when we arrived there at 4 a.m. that we hired a car and drove straight to the shores of the Sea of Galilee. There we watched numerous small boats, using lights, pulling out Peter's Fish on handlines. They were the local delicacy and we sampled them, barbecued, and enjoyed them very much.

Unfortunately my ankles then swelled up to mammoth size, just as they had done at Lake Rudolf, and took several hours to return to normality. I took the advice of an Israeli doctor and when I told him about my experience with the Nile perch he produced a fascinating geological and biological explanation.

Israel is the northernmost point of the Rift Valley which starts in East Africa. Eons ago, the Sea of Galilee and Lake Rudolf were part of the Rift Valley and their fish are closely related. The Peter's Fish, *Tilapia galilea*, is a pygmy compared with its colossal cousin, the Nile perch, *Tilapia nilotica*, but,

145

as I can testify, it packs the same punch for those allergic to that genus.

———————————◦———————————

Probably the most unpleasant example of fish affecting humans physically is the following story from the **Hon. Colin Orr-Ewing**.

My friend Vane Ivanović is renowned for his spear-fishing expertise and athletic ability, having represented his native Yugoslavia in the 1936 Berlin Olympics, both in water polo and hurdling. One day, while diving off Formentor in Majorca, he speared a blackfish, of about a pound in weight, and reached for the ring on which the catch is usually carried. Unfortunately, the ring had fallen away so Vane stuffed the dead fish down the front of his swimming trunks and returned to the shore.

Several weeks later he developed a skin rash in an embarrassing place, visited his doctor and was sent on to a specialist. With considerable professional excitement, the specialist eventually informed him that he was suffering from a form of ringworm peculiar to fishes and never, so far as the expert knew, found on a human being before.

'It is my duty to report this event in *The Lancet*, for the benefit of other doctors and their patients,' the specialist explained. 'May I have your permission to use your name, Mr Ivanović, and perhaps call the condition after you?'

Vane declined this dubious medical honour but, thereafter, paid close attention to any slap in the belly from a wet fish.

———————————◦———————————

It is now standard practice for serious anglers who pursue so-called coarse fish to release everything they catch, however large. What was then the British record carp, 44 pounds, was released into the aquarium at the London Zoo where it lived happily until it died a natural death. A close competitor, which has already been captured three times, holds what is likely to be an all-comers' record for the most valuable freshwater fish of all time, as **Bernard Aldrich** explains.

One of the artificial lakes at Stratfield Saye, the Duke of Wellington's estate in Berkshire, was held in place by a clay dam, in which a young tree had been allowed to establish itself. By the time of the great hurricane in 1987 the tree had reached such a size that it was blown down, bringing half the dam with it. So much water escaped from the lake that only a shallow and muddy remnant remained and something of quite extraordinary size was seen to be wallowing in it. It turned out to be a carp, in excellent condition, which turned the scale at a colossal 37 pounds – not a record fish but a specimen if ever there was one.

The fish's exact age was known because the lake had been stocked with carp twenty-six years previously and this had to be one of the originals. Since a carp can live to forty years or more there was plenty of life left in the monster, which would obviously be of value to lakes which let coarse fishing on a commercial basis. There is nothing like the certain knowledge that a lake contains a monster fish to bring queues of people wanting to catch it, photograph it and then return it to the water to fight another day.

With good commercial sense, the Stratfield Saye estate therefore decided to sell the fish and, after due publicity, there was so much interest that it was virtually auctioned. My employer, Lord Romsey, had opened a 27-acre lake as one of the countryside attractions at Broadlands and stocked it with coarse fish. He decided to bid for the carp and obtained it for the enormous price of £2,000. We called the fish Penny, which is splendidly inappropriate since it must be the world's most expensive freshwater fish.

At the time of writing Penny has more than earned the investment and its keep. From the moment it was lovingly placed in the lake, people have come from miles to try and catch it. Two have succeeded so far and others have hooked it without success. Penny always puts up a great fight and, so far, has been none the worse for being caught and returned. It continues to grow and if it lives long enough it might exceed the British record, which stands at 52 pounds. And the bigger it gets the more people will want to pit their wits against it.

***

Carp seem to be specially adept at hiding themselves and a whole population can exist in quite a small lake without anyone being aware of it, as my husband, **Harry Chapman Pincher**, describes.

When you are fishing, even when sport is poor, the odds are that the water, whether it be river or lake, holds many more fish than you imagine. The extraordinary ability to hide themselves possessed by quite large fish was demonstrated in a manner I have never forgotten during an early-morning visit to a small lake near Farnham, in Surrey.

I had lived near this quite shallow lake, called the Lodge Pond, for several years and used it for catching small pike baits when I rented some excellent pike water elsewhere. Before sunrise, in late August, I approached the pond, armed with a trout fly rod, light float tackle and a few small worms. The lake was shrouded in mist and from some distance I could see a large number of fairly small black objects moving slowly over the surface. I thought they must be frogs or toads but when I reached the edge I realised that they were the mouths of large carp which were audibly sucking in air.

According to the information supplied by the coarse-fishing section of the Farnham Anglers, to which I belonged, the Lodge Pond did not contain any carp so I was quite astonished by the sight before me. Some of the carp were very large – up to twenty pounds. Inevitably, I forgot about the pike baits and set about interesting the carp in my worms. There was no problem. In three hours, before I ran out of worms, I caught seventeen of them with a calculated weight of about ten stones! The biggest was a 12 ½-pound mirror carp. I know because I took it, along with four others I fear, being convinced that unless I did so and photographed them, nobody would believe me.

It took me a long time to play the fish because of the lightness of the tackle and the biggest kept me going for about twenty minutes.

When I reported the catch, along with the photograph, to Mr Albert King, the delightful club secretary who used to write to me 'Dear Coarse Member. . .', he confirmed that though the pond was well patronised nobody had ever caught a carp there or knew of their existence.

My husband's discovery no doubt induced a few keen carp fishers to try their luck in the Lodge Pond. Another instance of a large fish being able to hide its existence resulted in the provision of sport for many thousands of anglers, as **Anthony Strick**, an Australian transport engineer, has kindly put on record for me.

On the face of it, few would choose Western Australia for the establishment of a trout fishery. Extremes of temperature and other weather conditions affect the flow of rivers and streams to a discouraging extent. In the height of summer, temperatures approaching or even exceeding 100° Fahrenheit may persist for weeks on end, reducing the upper reaches, and much of the middle reaches, to a trickle between a series of stagnant pools. Winter rains result in widespread flooding and the main rivers may rise as much as 10 feet. But there is at least an abundance of food in the form of minnows and other small native fish, shrimps and marron, a freshwater crayfish indigenous to Western Australia which grows to a large size. No native species of fish are competitive.

Sporadic attempts to introduce brown trout in Western Australia were made at various times up to the early 1930s but none seems to have been successful. In 1931, however, a small group of enthusiasts made a determined attempt to rectify this unsatisfactory state of affairs: a proper hatchery was constructed and a consignment of brown trout ova was brought in by the newly inaugurated air service. The resulting fry were released in carefully selected feeder streams and the outcome was eagerly awaited.

For five long years nothing more was seen or heard of this release. Various fish were brought in from time to time for identification, but none of them looked like a trout. It was beginning to look as though the local conditions were too much for *Salmo trutta* when in 1936 a farmer reported the presence of a large and unusual-looking fish in a pool in one of the feeder streams. After an hour-long chase, the fish was finally captured, bundled ignominiously into an old hip-bath full of water and borne in triumph to the old hatchery. It was a brown trout of 11 ¼ pounds and in superb condition. Later a scale reading showed the fish to be five years old. The Jonahs were confounded and the enthusiasts vindicated. The construction of a new hatchery and a series of holding ponds was put in hand at once.

This one huge fish was the turning-point for trout fishing in Western Australia. Today, fifty years on, we have a trout fishery which can well be called unique. A beneficient government has taken over the running of the hatchery and holding ponds and restocks the rivers with brown and rainbow fry to compensate for the lack of spawning facilities and offset any losses due to high water temperature. A number of irrigation reservoirs are also regularly stocked and provide excellent fishing when the rivers are too low in summer. What we may lose in quantity is more

150

than made up in quality in both size and succulence – trout feeding on crayfish being something special for the gourmet. Four- and five-pounders are by no means uncommon, with the chance of double-figure fish in the larger rivers. The last two hundred fish taken by the writer and his wife have averaged a shade over 2 pounds, the largest being 7 ¼. Furthermore, it is all free; no licence is required and access to most waters is virtually unrestricted.

One cannot help wondering what might have happened, or rather what might not have happened, if that first big one had got away.

***

While it is usual for highly edible game fish, like salmon and trout, to end up on the table rather than back in the river, I have been told of several instances where a fish fought so gallantly that its captor returned it to fight another day. I witnessed one such event, my husband being the angler, and the fish being doubly lucky that day.

While nymphing for trout in August on the Littlecote water of the Kennet I hooked a large rainbow at about 5 p.m. It gave me the best battle I have ever had with such a fish and I was so impressed with its determination to survive that I decided that I would let it go if I managed to net it. I eventually landed it and, while gently removing my fly, I noticed another nymph, tied like a small pink shrimp, on the other side of the trout's mouth. I removed that too and after holding the fish in the current, watched it swim away, almost cheering it as it went. It was a superbly proportioned fish and could not have weighed less than six pounds.

I recognised the little shrimp as a pattern regularly used by one of the few ladies who fish the beat and put it in my fly box. About an hour later the lady came up the bank and

I asked her if she could remember losing a big rainbow in that area on one of her shrimps. She did and when I told her I had recovered her fly she predicted that there would be about an inch of nylon still attached to it because her cast had broken during a good fight. I gave her the fly and, sure enough, it was exactly as she had described it.

I then asked her when she had lost the fish. She had lost it at about 1.30 *that same day* – less than four hours before it greedily took my nymph.

That story disposes of the myth that trout will not rise again once they have been hooked and played and is good evidence in favour of the growing practice of catch–and–return on trout waters. Many anglers must have had similar experiences, but how many can match the following story, supplied by **Sir Denis Mountain**?

Flyfishing from a boat on the Spey in August I hooked a red salmon and, as it was going to be difficult to land, I decided to put the gillie in the stern and stand on the planking in the bow. As I manoeuvred the fish towards the net I saw that it was on the dropper fly. 'Be careful of the tail fly,' I called.

The sixteen-pounder came beautifully into the net and as the gillie put the net and the fish into the bottom of the boat he cried, 'Dammit, the tail fly's away.'

'Impossible,' I commented. 'It must be in the net.' The dropper was in the roof of the fish's mouth and the nylon, without a fly, was dangling below its tail.

'Look at that!' said the gillie, holding open the salmon's mouth. The tail fly was down its throat and the nylon we had seen was a long loop.

Presumably the fish had taken both flies in quick succession. It seems inconceivable that it would have taken the

152

second fly while it was being played. On the other hand, in fishing anything seems possible.

Derek Hallum, an Ipswich businessman, had a similar experience at sea.

I was fishing in a party of four off Cairns, in Queensland, in 1987. The marlin were out of season but we were trying for sailfish and other game species, some thirty miles out in the Pacific. There were four rods trailing baits behind the boat – one allotted to each of us. As soon as a fish struck at one of the baits, the other rods were required to reel in their baits as quickly as possible to prevent fouling of the lines.

Sport was good and we had caught tuna, shark and several other fish in the morning. At about 1.30 a lively fish struck at the outrigger bait on the starboard side of the boat and the angler began to play it. I reached for the rod attached to the outrigger bait on the port side and began to wind in the reel. Almost immediately I felt a good pull and with a cry of 'I've got one too' I began to play the fish.

After a couple of minutes both us began to realise that something was amiss. My line and that of the other rod were not only remarkably close together but our fish seemed to be moving as one. We soon realised that they were, indeed, moving as one because we were both playing the same fish. As my companion had hooked it first I took just a passive role and let him play it. Eventually he boated a twenty-pound dolphin-fish, which had both baits firmly in its mouth.

The dolphin-fish is ugly in shape, with a strange square head, but is magnificent in colour – a brilliant lemon-yellow with an electric blue tinge. This one must have been unusually hungry or, possibly, snapped at my bait out of aggression or frustration at already being hooked.

Clearly anything is possible with fishing, but who would believe that anyone would ever land a salmon in a pheasant covert? It happened to **Lord Brabourne.**

Some years ago, in March, I was fishing on the Avon near Christchurch, Hampshire, after there had been very heavy rainfall for several weeks. The river was very high and over its banks in many places. My host told me that it was impossible to fish but that I was welcome to try, so I set out with a spinning rod and a bait which looked rather like a herring.

I went to a pool where I had been successful in the previous year and all the surrounding fields were so covered in water that it was difficult to find a path to it. After a few minutes' fishing I hooked a salmon which was obviously of good size. It was very active and after swimming in the river for about ten minutes it suddenly decided to take off across the fields.

I ran after it, wearing thigh waders, with the water well above my knees. It went under a barbed-wire fence, which I managed to negotiate, and then, to my horror, under another barbed wire fence into a wood! The fish then swam into a bramble bush in which the cast became hopelessly entangled. It thrashed about for a bit but I was able to get to it, fall on it and eventually dispatch it. It weighed 29 ½ pounds and had given me the most unusual experience of my fishing career.

It was fitting that it should be Lord Brabourne who had that extraordinary encounter because, as an expression of his skill with both rod and gun, the late Lord Mountbatten once described him to my husband as 'half a fish and half a pheasant'. Another friend who is legendary for his fishing skill is **Barry Black,** of whom it has been said that he could catch a salmon in a

ploughed field. I have watched him on the Tay and such is his skill with the fly rod that nothing would surprise me. Here is his own story of 'The Nicotine Salmon'.

On a bright sunny day in 1937 I was fishing the Rest pool on the River Langa in Iceland. This is a very attractive long streaming pool, widening towards the tail, and is the nearest holding pool to the sea. The water was low but I knew that there were fresh fish in the pool, mostly grilse.

At some point I chucked the end of my cigarette into the stream and, out of the corner of my eye, I was vaguely aware that something unusual had happened in the water below me. It was just enough to make me follow my next cigarette end with my eye as it danced down the stream. It was there, then suddenly it was not there, and I though I saw a nose appear very gently where it had been. Could it be? Surely not! And yet! .... I broke another cigarette into pieces and threw them, one by one, into the river. This time there was no doubt: three pieces disappeared.

With the prospect of fishing dry fly for salmon, something novel in those days, I dashed back to the lodge on my pony (those marvellous ponies were one of the joys of fishing in Iceland then) to collect my 9-foot dry-fly rod and some old hackle Mayflies.

By the time I got back the sun was off the water but everything else looked the same. Full of hope, I waded in at the bottom of the pool and cast my mayfly upstream to where these fish had been. It floated down beautifully but nothing happened. I tried it again and again but it was no good. Further experiments on later days were more successful, however, and two things became clear – first, it was essential that the sun should be shining on the water; second, that the salmon always preferred cigarette ends to flies! Looking back now, I cannot think why I did not have the gumption just to try a cigarette end impaled on a hook. I suppose I thought it would be too much like a bait.

I tried the cigarette treatment on many other rivers but without much success. Perhaps I never found the right combination of factors again - bright sun on the water and a concentration of very fresh fish in a comparatively confined space. Perhaps I no longer used the right brand of cigarette – I used to smoke Turkish.

A similar incident was witnessed by **Ken Robinson** on the River Lune, where a group of anglers were gathering on a bridge, some to go salmon fishing on one beat, others to pursue the coarse fish on another. A large salmon had been spotted from the bridge and one of the coarse fishermen began to float wasp grubs over it to see what it would do. It took, then immediately released, nine wasp grubs before it tired of the game.

Salmon stomachs are almost invariably empty, but **Bernard Aldrich** assures me that he examined one from a fish caught on the Test and it was stuffed with may-flies.

It was a great pity that Barry Black did not become the first man to catch a salmon on a cigarette butt. It would have been a splendid example of improvisation but, perhaps, no more remarkable than that demonstrated by **Lord Home of the Hirsel**.

Lord Home is a tremendous walker and his younger brother, William, the playwright, has told me how he has often been exhausted trying to keep pace with him. So it was no surprise to me when Lord Home told me a salmon-fishing story which had resulted from the fact that he had walked four miles to a river carrying his rods.

When he arrived at the pool he intended to fish he felt in his pocket and found that he had left both his fly and bait boxes behind and it was too far, even for him, to walk back for them. He found a hook embedded in his hat and he also had a pocket-knife.

'I carved four pieces of driftwood into the shapes of minnows and had four salmon within an hour,' he told me.

That was improvisation! How many would have thought of doing it?

Lord Home did not explain how he carried four salmon home over four miles but, presumably, he did so – probably on a pole cut from a bush with his penknife and carried over his shoulder.

Sir Hector Laing, who owns a splendid stretch of the Findhorn, told me how, on an occasion when there were literally hundreds of salmon cruising round in a pool without one being a taker, the head gillie, who was fishing it, picked up a rock and threw it in with a mighty splash. When asked why he had done this the gillie replied, 'To rustle the buggers up.' That improvisation ploy did not work. Neither did a more sophisticated ruse by my husband on the South Esk.

An avid collector of fishing lore, he had read that poachers were occasionally in the habit of tying a light rope to a dead cat and pulling it through a salmon pool where they had placed a net. Believing the cat to be an otter, the fish were supposed to try to quit the pool and then entangle themselves in the net.

The trouble with the South Esk beat which my husband was going to fish was that the bulk of the salmon collected in a pool below a weir, and in the past he had tried throwing in stones to frighten some of them back to the lower pools. Being unwilling to operate with a dead cat, he made a toy one, as lifelike as he could, during the winter months and took it up to Scotland in April. It certainly frightened some fish out into the lower pools but the rather ridiculous effort was wasted because they would not take there either.

Much more successful was the ingenious improvisation devised by a charming river keeper whose writings have given pleasure and knowledge to many anglers.

Frank Sawyer was more than a fine fisherman, outstanding river keeper and innovator who invented the Pheasant Tail Nymph. He was a man of considerable ingenuity, as witness the story he told my husband when he was fishing a beat of the Hampshire Avon as a guest of the delightful Sir Grimwood Mears, who had first induced Frank to write his splendid books.

There had been an old brown trout, about a five-pounder, which had been hooked many times but had always escaped and, it seemed, always would. Its lie was a couple of yards above an iron grill leading to a sluice, through which the water swirled into a pool several feet below. As soon as it was hooked the trout disappeared between the bars of the grill down into the pool and no fisherman could follow it. A break always ensued.

Sir Grimwood asked Frank to catch it because, as he put it, the trout was undoubtedly eating its grandchildren. Frank fished for it until he hooked it and stripped off his fly line as fast as he could so that the trout escaped into the pool below without breaking the cast. Once he had reached the backing he cut it at the joint and attached the fly line to a large pike float which he had in his pocket for the purpose. With his rod tip he guided the float through the bars of the grill and then raced down to the pool.

When the float reached the end of the pool he fished it out, retied the line to his backing, tightened on the fish, which was still attached, and played it to the net.

Sometimes when a fish rushes through an obstacle or digs itself into a weed-bed steady pressure and patience will do the trick, as **Richard Adams,** the author of *Watership Down,* relates.

A few years ago I was fishing in Virginia with a friend, a local attorney named Tom Lawson. We were on a brook called Barbour's Creek, a very pleasant little stream about the size of the lower Lambourn in Berkshire. The banks are lined with trees in many places so that one needs to wade upstream.

Dusk was falling and there wasn't much time left when Tom came downstream to find me. 'Richard,' he said, 'there's a particular trout I would like you to try for. It's something a bit unusual. I'll show you what I mean.'

I followed him upstream to a pool which was closed off at the top by a slab of concrete wide enough to enable cars to cross the brook. Three covered culverts in it took the water from the pool above. 'Now,' said Tom, 'there's a good trout just upstream of the concrete but if you have a look at him you are certain to put him down. If I get into the undergrowth I shall be able to see the pool and tell you what to do.'

I was casting blind into the pool above and couldn't see my fly. 'A bit further to the right next time,' Tom called as I recovered the fly. I did as I was told and heard Tom shout, 'Strike.' I did so and could feel that the trout was on. I climbed out on to the concrete to get a tight line but the trout knew a trick worth two of that and bolted down out of sight into one of the culverts. I checked him to keep him in the culvert in the hope of drawing him back, knowing that he was lost if he reached the pool below, but he just stayed there in the gathering darkness. My cast was too fine to draw him out by force against the fast water so I just stood with the rod bent double.

Eventually, after about ten minutes, the trout gave up and I was able to draw him back into the upper pool, where Tom netted him. He weighed three-quarters of a pound – a good fish for that stream – and I had him for breakfast next morning, sitting on Tom's verandah close under the line of the Blue Ridge Mountains.

An Australian angler, **John Sautelle**, showed a similar determination to capture a fish for the table.

On my first evening's fishing in New Zealand, on Lake Waitaki in the South Island, we needed a good trout for supper and I was determined that it would be my first New Zealand fish that would be on the menu. Wading well out in shallow water and fishing a wet fly I was soon into a nice brown trout of about 3 ½ pounds — just what was required.

I was about to kill the fish and remove the fly when it gave a kick, broke the leader and fell into the water. With the air rather blue I prepared to put on another fly when I saw a trout's tail protruding from a tussock just below me. Using my almost forgotten tickling skill I managed to grasp the fish and saw my fly in its mouth.

Making no mistake a second time, I despatched it to cries from my friends that it should be put back since it had been caught illegally. However, they shared in the enjoyment of my first 'Kiwi' trout later that night for it was the only fish taken by the party.

Like Frank Sawyer, many anglers have contributed to the general store of knowledge of river and riverside natural history and several have sent me observations worthy of record, The one from **Sir Eric Faulkner**, a former chairman of Lloyds Bank, is especially remarkable.

Many years go I used to fish in the Elan valley in the Middle March of Wales. Being interested in its history, I read a good many books, including the Travels of Giraldus Cambrensis, a monk who was born at Manobier in the twelfth century. Giraldus describes a small lake high in the hills between the abbeys of Strata Florida and Cwmhir where the trout were pale of flesh on one side of the body but salmon-pink on the other. The lake is three or four miles from a road but in the 1930s I trekked up there to fish and, sure enough, the trout were still pink on one side and white on the other.

So fish and fishing do not change all that much over the centuries.

With his insatiable curiosity and unusual powers of observation and deduction, **Professor R. V. Jones**, who is a physicist, not a biologist, has come up with an observation of great interest to trout fishermen and fishery managers.

One of the great attractions of the upper Don at Corgarff, in Aberdeenshire, when we first had a house there in 1955, was the fishing. Although the river was no more than seven or eight yards wide, at its widest, it teemed with brown trout, all completely wild, and you could be sure of catching your breakfast day after day – except when a spate had left the fish so replete that they would not look at a fly, a minnow or even a worm.

One morning I encountered another angler – Charles Gibb, the son of the tenant farmer on the opposite bank. Like his father, who was a retired gamekeeper, he knew the river well. Of physical rather than intellectual bent, his mastery of the English language sometimes emulated that of Mrs Malaprop. His wife had been a cook at one of the big houses and there was an occasion before a grand dinner when she had been so proud of the setting of the table that she had smuggled Charlie in to see it. Afterwards he regaled us with the sight, ending with 'and in the middle of the table there was a great silver latrine for the soup'.

It was another of Charlie's observations which led me to serious thought. It came when we were both lamenting that the river was not so prolific as it used to be. 'It's the dam at Poldullie!' he said. 'The river has never been so good since they put up the dam.'

Now Poldullie was a good nine miles downstream and a dam had been built there for a private hydroelectric scheme. There was an over-steep fish ladder there intended for running salmon but Charlie said that the trout as well as the salmon were scarcer. I began to wonder whether trout were perhaps not quite so sedentary as I had hitherto imagined. Could it be that they too ran up and down river like salmon. Then I remembered that all the big trout I had caught (two-pounders) had been taken early or late in the season. This could be explained if they came to us for spawning in the autumn and them migrated downstream for feeding in the late spring.

The more I thought about this theory the more it appealed. After all, salmon, sea trout and brown trout are all the same family. I also knew of slob trout, which migrate up and down estuaries, changing from brown to silver in the process. Moreover, while fishing the Tongareiro in New Zealand, I learned that rainbow trout drop into Lake Taupo for summer feeding and return upstream in the autumn, when a spate brings them leaping back like running salmon.

Final proof came one November at Corgarff when Laurence Pilkington, of the famous glass firm, came to see me. The friends with whom he had been staying had a house near the very dam that had been the cause of Charlie's remark and they had been watching the ladder to see whether any salmon were running. There were very few salmon but, to their astonishment, there was a continuous succession of brown trout attempting the ladder – and some even succeeding. So brown trout *do* migrate like their cousins. Charlie had been right. May that dam, some day, be demolished!

The brown trout has been widely studied by scientists but there are still unrecorded aspects of its behaviour to be discovered by the observant angler, as the following event demonstrates.

On a summer evening in the early 1980s a member of the group which has the good fortune to fish the Littlecote beat of the River Kennet spotted a large trout behaving peculiarly, close in to the bank in water about five feet deep. He called my husband over to witness what was happening.

A male trout of about five pounds was shaking his head from side to side and firmly clamped across his jaws was a large grayling. For about ten minutes they watched while the trout' behaved like a dog playing with a bone, for it made no attempt to swallow the grayling. The trout then moved upstream, still carrying its prize, and continued what appeared to be its enjoyment. Some ten minutes later the grayling floated to the surface and was netted out by my husband from a convenient bridge. It weighed 1 ¼ pounds and there was hardly a mark on it. Perhaps the trout had not caught and killed it but picked it up when it was dead for what we would call fun.

───────◦───────

The trout in on Australian lake certainly interest themselves in very strange objects, as **Peter Hutley**, a British entrepreneur who has large interests in that country, has witnessed.

Whilst visiting Australia I took the opportunity to fish Lake Eucombean in the Snowy Mountains, having heard that it contained many large rainbow trout. The lake had been artificially created in a rocky valley and, as often happens in newly made waters, the fish had grown exceptionally rapidly.

I arrived with my elegant fly tackle and was soon joined by a friendly local inhabitant, who quickly assured me that I would not catch anything of any size with it. He then set up a heavy rod with a strong line ending in a very heavy lead weight with a large hook attached to it. Standing on the bank, he threw the lead out by hand into the water, which was about twelve feet deep, then, using the rod, he proceeded to bounce it up and down between the rocks.

'The big trout live on the bottom and they are attracted by the creatures I stir up out of the mud,' he explained. 'Eventually, one of them will have a go at the lead.'

It seemed a most unlikely method because there was nothing whatever in the way of bait on the hook, bait presumably being barred. Nevertheless it worked. While I caught only a few 8-ounce fish he produced a fat 4-pounder.

John Sautelle found himself similarly engaged in New South Wales.

I was sitting on a lake shore fishing for bream with hand lines with the lady who was to become my wife. Our baits – prawns – were laid on the bottom about six feet apart.

My line began to move and I was hooked into a good fish. As I began to retrieve it my fiancée called out 'I've got one too!' Eventually we landed our catches – the same fish, a black bream of two pounds which had taken both baits.

Ed Gardyne, a water engineer who now works on Deeside, passed on a most extraordinary observation which fits in perfectly with scientific findings on salmon migration.

It has been well established, by tagging experiments in Britain and America, that salmon not only return to the river of their birth to spawn but to the same tributary and even the same creek. If fertilized eggs are transferred to another river and allowed to hatch there then the salmon will return to that stream and not to the river where the eggs were laid. So it seems certain that it is after hatching that the particular quality of the water surrounding them is somehow imprinted on the little fish and is remembered for ever.

Experiments also suggest that it is through the sense of smell that adult salmon find their way back to their special water and, having detected the right river, they press on until they find their hatching place.

This would seem to be the only explanation for a most remarkable event which happened at the salmon hatchery at Eskadale on Lord Lovat's estate in Scotland. The water for the hatchery was drawn from a tributary of the Beaulieu river through a pipe and, after passing through the hatchery, was discharged through another pipe into the main river. Occasionally, tiny salmon escaped into the river or were deliberately put in there for stocking.

One morning the whole hatchery was found to be flooded and, clearly, there had been a blockage of the exit pipe. Various inspection manholes were examined and it soon became obvious that the blockage must be near the point where the exit pipe entered the Beaulieu. Chest waders were donned and a workman slid his hand up the pipe and pulled out a large salmon. He repeated this several times and finally the water began to flow freely again.

There was no doubt that the salmon had quite deliberately swum up the pipe with such determination that they had blocked it and, since this is not their normal practice, it is a fair assumption that they were drawn there by the particular quality of the water in the hatchery where, presumably, they had emerged from eggs several years before.

As my husband began his professional life as a biologist, he has maintained his interest in natural history and recorded his more unusual observations. On one occasion when he was fishing a stream on the River Tees, while it was slightly flooded, he noticed a rabbit hop across a sandbank towards the water's edge within five yards of him and watched it, thinking that it must be wanting a drink.

To his astonishment, the rabbit sat for a few moments and then very deliberately entered the water, swam out into the stream, paddled about there for a while and then swam back again. It rested on the sandback, shook off its excess water, as a dog would, and then hopped back into a wood. In all his hundreds of hours spent by the waterside my husband has never seen a rabbit swim on any other occasion. He has, however, one other rabbit story connected with fishing.

When he was young he had been ferreting on the riverbank near the village of Croft, where he lived. It was the practice to gut the rabbits before taking them home and the entrails were simply thrown into the water to get rid of them. The water was soon aboil with huge chub tearing at the unexpected offering and no doubt attracted from their lairs by the smell of it.

Not one to waste such a windfall of knowledge, Harry tried rabbit gut as a bait in a chub hole, dropping in the main part of the gut attached to a stone to attract the fish and putting a couple of inches of small intestine on a large hook. It worked and he was soon into a chub of four pounds, quite large for that river, and caught several more.

It was a rather larger and, sadly, rarer creature than a rabbit which intruded itself into the notice – and into the sport – of **Jack Coates**, the current Chairman of the Salmon and Trout Association.

An invitation to stay at Upper Suisgill in May and fish the Helmsdale was the fulfilment of a long-held dream. Having just returned, jet-lagged, from Australia, however, I did not enjoy the long drive north, nor was I thrilled on arrival when our enthusiastic gillie, Donald, suggested that, as the river was running down and conditions were bright, two of us should start fishing at 5 a.m. each day! But the magic of that beautiful glen soon washed away the fatigue and our party set about its task with vigour.

By the end of the week we had landed seven fish and lost a few more, which was about par for the course that season. We had tramped and scrambled over most of the twenty miles covered by the beats, usually casting into the teeth of a brisk easterly wind, yet spurred on by that infinite capacity for anticipation which is so essential for salmon fishing. Indeed, in May, this wasn't a difficult place in which to enjoy a blank day: clusters of stags cropping the new spring grass among the birch trees; the almost invisible nests of sandpipers and other waders to be avoided on the shingle banks; and, occasionally, the sight of a hen harrier quartering the moor looking for young grouse.

On the last bright morning, with the need for another fish a high priority. I was asked to go with Donald to walk all the way down to the lowest beat, known as One Below, where there was the best chance of a fresh fish. It was marvellous water, with fast-running streams and holding places every hundred yards or so, in all about two miles long. As the morning went by, eager anticipation gave way to dogged determination, encouraged by a continuous input of information from Donald. Then at last, towards the tail of the penultimate pool, known as the Whinnie, he said quietly, 'I think a fish moved.' On

168

casting again there was no doubt about it – a bulge but no contact. Trembling, as is usual in such moments, I made the third cast and bang – the fish came in earnest, but miserably I failed. Desperately disappointed but with characteristic Highland courtesy, Donald said, 'That was a difficult fish; we'll give it a rest for a while.'

When we returned all was quiet and I suggested that Donald should show me how to do it. We crouched down the bank while he selected a small fly of his own tying. As he was just about to cover the lie I saw something every strange in the shallows below the lip of the pool, like a stick waving gently from side to side. Nearer it came until we realised that it was the tail of an otter, busily hunting up the stream. 'Sod's Law', muttered Donald, but I was transfixed by the sight of this beautiful creature coming over the lip of the pool, straight towards our salmon lie. Being short-sighted, he hadn't seen us and dived under water. There was an almighty swirl and then silence. What went on down there I can only guess but, after a few seconds, up came Tarka, whiskers glistening and, I am sure, with a grin on his face. Then he winded us, only ten yards away, and sank out of sight into the now fishless lie.

Frustrated, we climbed up the bank without our last fish, but, in spite of its high priority, I shall never forget the joy that otter gave me. After all, it was more his river than mine.

———————————⟫◦⟪———————————

Barbara Hawkins witnessed a similar incident.

A year or two ago I was fishing with a friend on Wester Elchies, a lovely beat on the left bank of the Spey just above Aberlour. On the opposite bank was a party of Frenchmen, one of whom was a stocky little man who fished with great enthusiasm, long after the gillie had

169

gone home. He was a competent fisher, using a 7-foot single-handed fly rod, and waded intrepidly without a stick in the strong and rocky water. He resolved the problem of how to land his fish without a gillie by summoning his poor wife and, after much frenzied shouting and changing of position, they usually managed.

One evening, when we were returning by the track alongside the Rhynd Pool we saw the unmistakeable figure, bobbing about and obviously into a substantial fish. The little rod was well bent but he seemed to be making no impression on the quarry, in spite of every angle and manouevre. He had already summoned his wife, who was standing with one of those large Spey nets designed for female gillies.

Eventually, after the usual stream of instructions, it was clear that they were gaining ground and we saw a large ripple approaching the outstretched net. However it was not a salmon that swam into the net but a large dog otter!

In great alarm, the Frenchman sprang out of the water, almost knocking his wife over, and scampered up the bank into some brambles, fortunately extracting the fly from the otter's back on the way.

General Sir David Thorne was impressed by a wild creature which intruded itself, equally effectively, into his fishing.

In September 1982, some two months after my arrival in the Falkland Islands, I decided to have a go at fishing, which I had never tried before. I was talked into it by Major Anthony Stansfeld, who was commanding an Army Air Corps squadron on a tour of duty in the islands.

After a thirty-minute helicopter flight we landed beside the upper waters of the San Carlos river which looked very peaty. Anthony explained how to cast but the pool he had selected looked utterly empty to me. As I reeled in the Mepps spoon there was a powerful pull and I could scarcely believe it when a 3 ½ pound sea trout eventually came to the net. One cast – one fish! What a sport!

I was rather disappointed when my next two casts produced nothing but, on the fourth, I had the exhilaration of fighting a 5 ½ pounder.

After that the sport suddenly ended because a large king cormorant had arrived and taken up a position on the far side of the pool. We then had the remarkable experience of seeing him chase a small sea trout across the stream. He missed it and rose out of the water looking furious, almost as though we had been responsible for his failure. As the rest of the fish had almost certainly been put down, we decided to leave him in peace in the pool where we were the interlopers.

That day was very memorable as my introduction to the marvellous sport of fishing. Oddly, though, my most vivid recollection of it is not the sea trout but the king cormorant looking at us, eye to eye, as an equal in his territory.

It was a substantially larger intruder that upset the fishing on the Nursling beat of the Test, as **Vic Foot**, the gillie there, recalls.

Although the side-stream of the River Test in which we catch most of our salmon at Nursling is not very wide, we do get some very large fish coming up on occasion and salmon weighing over forty pounds have been caught. Such big fish move a lot of water when they swim upstream and the bow-wave I saw one day while on the tidal part of the river made me think that we had a real monster coming in. I followed it with my eyes, still wondering about its size, when it heaved itself out of the water and I saw that what we had was no salmon but the salmon's worst enemy (next to poachers), a seal. It lurched itself out onto the bank but when it saw me approaching it slid back in and went further upstream. Apparently it decided to stage its circus act because within a few moments it reappeared with a sea trout in its mouth, threw the fish into the air, caught it, and dived without waiting for my applause.

I followed it upstream for about half a mile wondering what it would do next. The salmon and sea trout – far more than I had believed were there – were rushing up and down the pools in panic. I realised that we would not be catching many of them while the seal was about so I tried to get above it in the hope of turning it, but it could swim against the current faster than I could run. I succeeded only because the seal was half-beached on a shallow section between two pools. It was determined to flop on upstream but by good fortune there happened to be a few bricks handy on the bank and I managed to bombard him. After taking a few direct hits he set off at tremendous speed back to the estuary, scattering a team of army frogmen who were clearing the bottom of poachers' tackle as an exercise. I have never seen soldiers move so fast.

A still larger creature intruded itself into a stream my husband was fishing.

One summer evening I was worm-fishing for trout in a clear, shallow stretch of the River Tees, near Croft Spa. Wading carefully in what was a favourite stream, I cast the worm so that the current swished it round the boulders. It was not long before there was a twitch and the very fine gut – it was before the days of nylon – moved upstream. Result – a fighting half-pounder, which was a nice fish for that stretch.

172

As I was rebaiting the double hook I heard the sound of a horse being ridden towards the river. The rider, a groom in breeches and rubber boots, dismounted, touched his bowler hat politely and then, to my astonishment, splashed into the water beside me, dragging the horse in after him. Every trout within a hundred yards must have heard the clatter of the horse's hooves as they slithered over the cobbles.

'What do you think you're doing?' I spluttered angrily.

'Just hardening the horse's legs, sir', the groom replied in a disarming Dublin brogue. 'Cold water is good for a steeplechaser's legs.'

I was about to curse him and all his Irish ancestors when I felt a sharp tug at the line, which was dragging in the water about ten yards downstream. I struck instinctively and the liveliest trout I had hooked that season leapt out of the water.

After a pantomime tussle in which the line became entangled round the horse's legs and the groom got one boot full of water, I netted the trout under the horse's nose. It weighed 1 pound 3 ounces.

While swans or Canada geese flopping down on to a pool can be a confounded nuisance, birds do not often intrude into our sport. However, the incumbent Poet Laureate, **Ted Hughes**, has sent me the charming details of two such incidents.

A few years ago I was trout fishing with my son on the River Barrow, in Ireland. We were not far apart but out of sight of each other, with trees and bushes between us. As I was casting, I hit a swallow with my rod tip – something which had never happened to me before or since. The bird dropped into the river, where it floated like a little boat with its head up. I tried to help it towards

173

the shore with my rod but it began to row itself, with flaps and flutters, directly towards me, till I was able to bend down and pick it up. I held it in my cupped, open hands, not knowing quite what to do, when, suddenly, it pulled itself together, launched itself into the air and flew off over the river as if nothing had happened.

I then waded upstream towards my son, partly, I suppose, to tell him about the curious happening, and met him coming round the corner downstream towards me. As I began to tell about the swallow, he fumbled inside his pullover and pulled out a swift. He had just knocked it out of the air while casting, and had fished it out of the river. He was now drying it. As he held it up to show me, it dipped out of his hands and flew away over the river.

I've often wondered, did our two separate rods connect with those two separate birds at precisely the same second? It was surely within the same minute and we were not more than thirty yards apart.

A swallow or a swift is too light to occasion much inconvenience but **Tommy Parrington**, the well-known fisherman and Shot, has told me how his late sister, Jean, was quietly fishing the Ness when a heron, probably taking evading action after suddenly seeing her, flew into electric wires above her and crashed down inches away. She was very frightened.

I have been struck by a bird, repeatedly, while fishing, or rather while trying to. It happened in Iceland, where I had been put on a wonderful pool called the Stone. This fishes all the way down but unfortunately it happened to be in the territory of an Arctic tern which had a nest on the cobbles. Every time I tried to wade into the water, the bird made a very determined attack to frighten me away. It was July and I was not wearing a hat. So, with the feminine dread of getting a bird or a bat entangled in my hair, I admitted defeat and moved far enough downstream to satisfy the tern.

175

Eventually, my husband appeared on the opposite side and needed to wade across, the only possible place being near the tern's nest. Though he waved his rod furiously at the attacking bird, he was continuously 'bombed', which was not pleasant when he was trying to negotiate the fast current.

He made it but the bird had made its point and won the contest. He did not wade across at that place again.

A certain angler, well known to me but who must be nameless here, was fishing for trout in a weir-pool on the River Kennet. The fish were feeding but so were several semi-tame mallard. In the course of casting towards a likely rise my friend hooked one of the ducks in a wing feather and he found himself playing a lively bird, loudly quacking its concern. No doubt this has happened before many times and would hardly be worthy of record except that, in this case, the duck decided to fly and the angler found himself playing a creature high over his head. His rod point was certainly well up but, inevitably, he suffered a broken cast and the loss of his Tup's Indispensable as well as dignity.

***

For accidental contact between a fly and another object the palm must surely be awarded to **John Fowles**.

After an enjoyable but otherwise unsuccessful day's salmon fishing in Scotland, our group gathered in the hotel for the evening. Having experienced somewhat rowdy fishing parties before, the manager had opened up the ballroom and given us the ballroom bar, in the corner.

As the evening wore on and more alcohol was consumed, the claims to casting prowess became wilder and wilder so, eventually, someone was dispatched to

collect a fly rod and a competition was organized on the ballroom floor, casting at various targets. One of those present was a former Scottish fly-casting champion and was beginning to irritate everybody. So, fortified more by spirit than by skill, I undertook to show him a thing or two.

We had been smoking cigars so I collected two of the metal containers and stood one on a shelf in one corner of the ballroom and the other on the floor in the corner diagonally opposite, intending to cast the fly at both in turn.

I stood in the middle of the room, with all watching, and, somewhat unsteadily the worse for drink, false-cast the line a few times and then shot the last few yards at the container on the shelf, knocking it off. Automatically I back-cast the line to recover it and in the process, and without turning round, knocked down the other container. It was a total fluke but there was a stunned silence, save for the footsteps of the Scotsman as he went to bed.

As the distance of the back-cast was some forty yards the odds against anyone being able to do that again must be enormous.

THE NINETEENTH POOL

In the way that golf club-houses are universally known as the Nineteenth Hole, perhaps good fishing pubs and fishing hotels catering for anglers should be referred to as the Nineteenth Pool. As all who stay in them know, achievements can be shared and celebrated there and sorrows drowned. Much laughter can also be generated, as **Professor R. V. Jones** recalls.

In one of his many interviews on television, the late Jimmy Edwards (better known as a comedian than as a holder of the Distinguished Flying Cross and a Cambridge degree) remarked on the recondite knowledge of some members of the academic community and illustrated his thesis by describing, his experience in an Aberdeenshire inn. Its bar had some fifty-five different brands of whisky on its shelves and he had been taken there by a professor who proceeded to offer him a drink. What impressed Jimmy was that none of the first three whiskies nominated by the professor was to be found among the fifty-five available and Jimmy could only speculate on how knowledge of such rarities had been acquired.

There is another side to this incident, for I was the professor concerned, and it was, in fact, angling that had led us, as angling so often does, to the bar. The year was 1958 but our acquaintance had started in 1952 when Jimmy had been elected as Lord Rector of Aberdeen University by the students, who rejoiced in the shock that the election of a comedian would give to the fustier members of the Senatus Academicus for, although elected by the students, the Lord Rector is by law the chairman of the governing body, the university court. And shock there certainly was – so much so that the Senatus and the students were soon at loggerheads. The students appealed to me for help, for they had observed that the one smiling face among the returning officers when a scowling vice-chancellor had announced the result of the election had been mine.

Suffice it to say that peace was ultimately made and Jimmy's rectorial address received the greatest publicity in living memory. He behaved tactfully as Rector, giving generously to student funds and making no attempt to intervene in university affairs other than to attend student functions, whenever invited. Although as a comedian he was regularly on tour, he never accepted a stage engagement in Aberdeen while he was Rector and it was only some years later that he agreed to appear. When this news reached the press he was asked whether, in view of his previous mixed reception at the university, there was anyone he looked forward to meeting again. He named me.

On reading that, I telephoned him, asking him whether there was anything he would like to do while he was in Aberdeen. He replied that he had never fished and would like to try. Fortunately, one of my friends had a beat on the River Don, just above Kemnay, and he gladly offered us hospitality.

I myself was only a moderate fisherman and so, to make sure that Jimmy would at least see a fish caught, I asked my good friend, Dr Archie Young, to come with us, for he was a fisherman of skill. I went to Jimmy's hotel to pick him up and, as he had a pressman in tow who had to write an article about him, I took him too.

We drove out to Kemnay to find Archie Young and our host already there, I set Jimmy up with a rod and we took our stations on the river. There was only an hour or so to go to lunch and in that time neither Jimmy nor I had a touch, though Archie had hooked a good trout only to lose it.

I had booked lunch at the Burnett Arms in Kemnay and it was in the bar there that the incident of the fifty-five whiskies occurred. We were the only patrons save for a morose-looking individual, who turned out to be a merchant seaman, sitting in a befuddled slough of despond after several days of heavy drinking. Gradually he awoke from his coma to find that he was looking at the well-known figure of Jimmy Edwards, whom he had often seen on television and in the cinema.

He struggled to his feet and lurched up to Jimmy saying, 'Man, ye're like Jimmy Edwards – but ye're nae as big.' The more that Jimmy insisted that he was the real Jimmy Edwards, the more the answer came – 'Ye canna be! Ye're nae as big.'

Ultimately Jimmy said, 'I'll prove it to you – I'll do anything you've seen Jimmy Edwards do!'

Jimmy was famous for a series of one-man sketches and our inebriated seafarer named one of them. Promptly, in front of all of us and the landlord, Jimmy did the entire turn in a corner of the bar, only to be met with 'Verra guid – but ye're still nae as big!'

Jimmy then drew himself up to his full height, inflated his lungs to their full volume, twitched his enormous moustache and did another complete turn. He put everything into it and was really very funny, but all to no avail – the seafarer was even fuller of appreciation than he was of alcohol, but always came the reproachful comment 'But ye're nae as big!'

After another two hilarious turns which delighted us, Jimmy had to give up and we went in to lunch. Neither Archie nor I caught anything in the afternoon but we heard a shout of 'Oy' that might have come from Jimmy's radio character Mr Glum. I looked upstream to see Jimmy in plus-fours and cloth cap standing in mid-river in a shallow run with something on his line. It was a 6-ounce trout and he seemed to have hooked it on a back-cast, for it was well behind him. His subsequent antics were even better than they had been in the bar. At times he was bent double, at others collapsing backwards, but he managed to keep his head and his footing as he splashed about with the trout swimming all around him. Several times I though he had lost it, so slack was the line, but the trout seemed bent on suicide and he ultimately landed it after a struggle that would have done credit to a 4-pound sea trout.

It was the only fish that any of us caught that day and a triumphant Jimmy made sure that the pressman got his story.

Occasionally, the Nineteenth Pool can be the site of dismay.

Tommy Parrington fished regularly on the great Spey beat called Delfur, as a guest of Sir Thomas Sopwith, along with my husband and the late Lord Dilhorne, then Lord Chancellor. On one bright day in April not a single fish had been caught until about 5.30 pm, by which time Sir Thomas and Lady Sopwith and the gillies had left the river.

Tommy then hooked a large salmon in a huge pool, called Beaufort, and, though on his own, managed to land it. It weighed 26 pounds and was in perfect condition – a model Spey springer fresh from the sea.

Understandably, Tommy took it back to the Craigel-lachie Hotel with some pride, placed it on the table in the small cool room set aside for salmon captured by the guests and, after washing and taking a cup of tea, went to Sir Thomas's bedroom to ask him to descend to view the catch which had prevented a blank day. Sadly the fish had vanished.

The staff were questioned, the police were called in, guests were accused of playing a joke, but the mystery was never solved. It seemed impossible that such a huge fish could have been spirited out of the front door or even a back door and the final view was that someone had swiftly handed it through the small window in the cool room to an accomplice who had rushed it away to some ready buyer.

What of the Lord Chancellor? His advice was sought but as the nation's top lawyer he felt it necessary to remain remote from such a minor case, which could well attract local publicity.

———————————⊃●⊂———————————

The ideal Nineteenth Pool is the great house or castle attached to a salmon beat, when one has been invited as a member of a fishing party. But this too can have its disadvantages.

Most salmon anglers would agree that if a large salmon is hooked it should be played until it is caught, even if it means staying by the river after darkness has fallen. A former owner of the Kinnaird estate, near Dunkeld, however, did not agree. This gentleman, the late Sir John Ward, was a stickler for manners and regarded being late for lunch as inexcusable, as it affected all the other guests. His gillies on his famous stretch of the Tay were, therefore, enjoined to warn any angler who was into a fish and unable to land it in time to make it back to the lunch table by 1 pm that they should break the line rather than give offence. Those who declined to do so were tactfully advised by the gillie that to be late to lunch for the sake of a salmon, however large, was to risk never being invited again. This has been confirmed to me personally by one of the old gillies involved.

Perhaps Sir John took this view because big Tay salmon were so common in those days. As I have already mentioned, several fish over forty pounds – all caught on fly – grace the walls of the billiard room at Kinnaird, which is now a hotel.

A forty-pound salmon is certainly worth setting up if wall-space is available and, in the course of my requests for stories, I have received accounts of many memorable fish. Sadly, there is room for only a small selection and pride of place must go to a fish hooked by **David Sussman** for which wall-space would *not* have been available.

The seas of Bazaruto Island, in the Mozambique Channel, are home to some of the world's largest bill-fish, and particularly the giant black marlin. In the 1950s and '60s,

185

when the change in the Humboldt current had destroyed the marlin waters off Cabo Blanco in Peru, and before the discovery of the incredible resources of Cairns, at the Australian Barrier Reef, Bazaruto was the only place in the world where fish over 1,000 pounds were known to exist.

Our base was the little island of Santa Carolina, known somewhat hopefully as Paradise Island, from which the five or six operable boats set out at six in the morning to round Barazuto, and to whose golden beach we returned just before sunset each evening. There was no radio communication but you began to see the gantry on the beach from some four or five miles out. If the marlin hanging there became visible when your boat passed a certain sand-bar, then you knew that a very large fish had been caught.

At the time of which I write a few dozen fine fish had been boated by dedicated anglers who, year after year, braved the primitive accommodation and the unreliable single-engined herring-boats, but the largest fish to have been weighed in was 920 pounds. Hard-luck stories abounded of huge marlin smashing line, rods, chairs and even boats, of record fish torn to the skeleton by sharks in the closing stages of the fight, and of on-and-off fish whose size melted the knees and dried the mouth. The magic 1,000-pounder was yet to be caught.

It was near the end of a ten-day expedition to the island that my friend Geoff and I were trolling our baits in the cobalt-blue water a mile or so to seaward of Barazuto itself. During the visit we had each boated a fish of about 400 pounds and lost a couple of similar size. Whatever lay ahead, we considered the trip to have already been successful.

We only reached the marlin grounds at midday, bait was scarce and we spent a couple of hours drifting past the reef at the northern tip of the island, casting and retrieving heavy spoons to catch half a dozen Spanish mackerel for the day's fishing. The tropical sun burned

186

down on us from directly overhead; there was only a tin canopy over the helmsman's stool on the open deck and we needed to cover ourselves thickly with sun lotion to avoid the third-degree burn which had ruined so many anglers' visits to the area.

It was vital to concentrate upon the two baits pulled from the outriggers, one short and one long, skipping and diving behind the slow-moving boat. If a marlin struck you had to be at the reel with gloved hand to stop the freely revolving spool from overrunning, gently enough for the fish to swallow the bait past the mouth and bill before it felt any unnatural pull and ejected it. On average, you could expect only one strike a day and the combination of the ferocious heat and the previous night's customary excess of vino tinto made concentration very onerous. Accordingly, one man fished both rods for an hour at a time, so that the other could rest his eyes and his skin from the glare of sun and sea.

It was my turn on the rods and, standing on the gently swaying deck next to the primitive fighting chair we had constructed, I thought I saw a dark shape some yards behind the far bait. I shouted in excitement. Geoff leapt to join me in the stern and the African skipper left his wheel to stand with us, staring. The shape had vanished, however, and the skipper returned to the helm, clucking disapprovingly. Geoff followed him under the canopy and I turned to light a cigarette and relax my burning eyes. As I did so I saw the short line pull out of its outrigger clip amidships. I rushed back to the chair only just in time to lightly palm the reel, which had begun to turn. I climbed into the chair, lifted the heavy rod and reel into the gimbal and fixed the clips of the seat-harness onto the reel lugs, all with my free hand. Geoff quickly reeled in the second bait and stowed the rod away and the skipper stopped the boat.

The line pulled out rapidly for a few seconds and then stopped.

'Shaka,' said the skipper, pessimistically.

'Not a shark,' I said in the pidgin Zulu in which we communicated. 'It's a marlin.'

We all held our breath. Was the fish turning the bait to swallow it and swim off or had it felt the great hook, just projecting from the stomach of the 8-pound Spanish mackerel, and disappeared into the depths? I pulled my glove on nervously and shifted in the chair. The boatman laid the flying gaffs under the gunwales and tied the ends of their 30-foot hawsers to the bollards. The sun beat down, the boat rolled and wallowed on the oily swell and I could hear my own heart beat.

After what seemed like an hour but could only have been a minute or so, the line started to move again, slowly at first but rapidly accelerating.

I flipped the gear on the heavy reel into its 40-pound drag and screamed at the skipper, 'Go, go, go!'

The boat lumbered into its 8-knot maximum speed, the 130-pound line lifted taut out of the water, the heavy rod bent almost double and I struck the fish three times as hard as I could to set the hook. The line screamed out – two hundred yards, three hundred yards and more until the reel began to smoke. I gradually released the drag and shouted to the captain to turn and run parallel to the fish so that I could recover line. The single-engined boat came about, the reel slowed down and stopped and I began to wind back some of the 500 yards of Dacron from the sea.

We had not yet sighted the fish but the speed of that initial run left no doubt that it was a marlin. I pumped the rod and wound the line back faster and faster, tightening the drag progressively. The chair was slowly turned to face the stern again and the line emerged from the clear blue water. Suddenly, about a hundred yards from the beam and just ahead of the boat, a massive marlin exploded through the surface. I could not believe it was the same fish until the line started to run out as the monster leapt again and again, nine great jumps, often clearing the water by its own length. At each jump we all cheered

188

as the marlin, with its mouth wide open and gills flaring, tried to shake the hook out.

As the fish greyhounded and tail-walked at incredible speed across the water, the helmsman pushed his rusty old diesel engine to its utmost to keep up and Geoff, who was guiding my chair, said in a whisper, 'Its huge, David, huge!'

Finally the fish sounded into the deep water and I settled down to the back-breaking task of pump and retrieve, sometimes an inch at a time, sometimes more, until every muscle hurt and I began to see blood.

An occasional sip of lukewarm water from Geoff was like nectar. He poured some over my hat and neck to cool me off, spread more sun lotion on my burning legs and forearms and eased the harness so that the taut straps cut me in stages and not in the same place. Whilst I pumped it shallower and shallower the fish was swimming slowly seaward, where, fortunately, there was less chance of encountering sharks.

After some forty minutes the red whipping, marking the start of the doubled-up line, emerged from the surface. That meant 30 feet of double line with an effective breaking strain of 260 pounds and then 30 feet of seven-stranded aircraft cable – only 60 feet between me and the fish and I could hardly bear to think of it.

The boatman, peering into the water, shouted, 'Yena makulu kakulu' – 'It's very big' – and Geoff left the chair for a second to see for himself.

'Oh my God!' he said when he returned to his post. 'It's a thousand pounds plus!'

With renewed strength, I inched the red whipping through the rod tip, down the ball-bearing runners on the heavily bent rod and, finally, onto the reel. With two or three turns of the double line safely on the reel I tightened the drag to its maximum. The fish and the boat were moving as one, at 3 or 4 knots. The rolling of the boat in the swell pulled a foot or two of line off the reel but allowed me to retrieve a little more as the stern dipped down again.

At last the big stainless-steel swivel attaching the double line to the trace-wire came slowly out of the water and I saw the fish through my misted-up Polaroids. Its tail and bill completely overlapped the width of the 10-foot stern and its back was as wide as a buffalo's. It had lit up and its great pectoral and dorsal fins were a blaze of fluorescent purples and blues. I had never seen anything so beautiful or so formidable.

The boatman, a slightly built Shangaan, rolled his eyes nervously at me and the skipper. 'You take it Geoff,' I said. 'I don't think he has the heart for it.'

Geoff pulled on a pair of heavy gloves and crouched at the transom with arms outstretched to grasp the trace and pull the fish to the gaff. The swivel inched up closer and closer until he was able to grab the cable, first with one hand then with the other. The muscles on his neck and shoulder stood out like whipcord as he pulled the giant fish, a foot or two at a time, towards the boat. The skipper left the engine ticking over and stood with the gaff next to Geoff. I released some of the enormous drag on the reel in case the fish made a run for it and stretched and bent my aching arms and legs in blessed relief. I called to the boatman to coil the 500-pound cable neatly on the deck as Geoff drew it in, but the heavy strain had removed some of its flexibility and it lay about, stiffly and untidily.

A sudden weary flip of the marlin's tail caused it to surge away and Geoff lunged out with it over the gunwales. 'Let go!' I shouted, and he did. The cable leapt up off the deck like a spring and I braced myself for the shock pull that followed. The cable came up taut and the fish took a few yards of double line from the reel. I winched it back without too much difficulty and Geoff prepared to grip the trace again. We were both horrified to see that a kink had been set in the stainless steel wire, about halfway down.

Geoff turned to me, silently, despairingly.

190

'You'll have to get it first time,' I said. 'Bring the kink inboard and then wrap the trace round a bollard so it can't run out.'

'I don't think I can pull it alone,' he said. 'There's a chance if the boatman helps me.'

The International Game Fishing Association, of which I was (and still am) the South African representative, lays down a series of stringent rules to ensure a fair contest between angler and fish. One of them, at that time, was that only one man at a time could take the trace.

I fleetingly weighed in my mind the choice between losing the biggest fish of my life and the ignominy of having caught it in breach of the rules, to which I fervently subscribed.

'No, Geoff,' I said. '*You* must do it.'

Again he gripped the trace, again he heaved and strained to draw the fish inwards and again the trace lay about the deck whilst the kink came closer and closer. There was a tiny flash down the taut wire as one of the seven strands broke at the kink. Would it last, I wondered, until the weak point was secured?

Moments later another strand broke away, followed by one more. The weak point was scarcely twelve inches from Geoff's hand but his strength was ebbing. He could hold the fish but not move it. He glanced over his shoulder at me, agonizingly, and as he did the wire snapped altogether. Geoff crashed to his back still holding the now unravelled end of the wire and I leapt to my feet to watch the great fish veer off and disappear into the deep. The skipper returned to the wheel, spun it hard over and set off for home, leaving a cloud of black smoke over the scene of the tragedy. None of us uttered a word.

But was it, I wondered, such a tragedy? I had hooked, fought and fairly brought to the boat one of the world's greatest game fish. As an angler I had done all I could. By staying within the rules I had, albeit involuntarily, given it its freedom to live on and thrive instead of bringing it to hang lifelessly from the gantry on the beach.

I repeated my thoughts to Geoff but he was not to be consoled. He lifted his face from his hands and said, 'But it was such a wonderful fish!'

The following year, on the island, I had the excitement of weighing in Ralph Hulett's 1,001-pounder, the first ever off the coast of East Africa. A few more have been caught at Barazuto since and the present record is Monty Smith's monster of 1,106 pounds. I myself have caught some forty marlin since and have released all but a couple of them. The largest, caught off Cairns, weighted about 950 pounds.

A year after my experience, the International Game Fishing Association amended the rule which led to the loss of my record fish and now allows more than one man to take the trace.

All of us who have lost big fish will appreciate David's feelings, and none more so than **Max Hastings**, whose *cri-de-coeur* follows.

There was a time when I thought of myself as a lucky salmon fisher. Not only did I hook fish when better men and women than I were failing to do so; I landed them. Admittedly, there was a week in Alaska when we were all connecting with so many fish that we became lazy about following them downstream, confident that even if we lost one there would be another along three minutes later. But in Scotland, almost without exception, when I felt the heart-stopping tug on the line I was pretty confident that I would have a fish on the bank.

About three years ago, however, all that began, dismayingly, to change. I started losing fish almost as fast as I hooked them, and very demoralizing this proved to be. It began on the first day of the week on the Naver, when after watching my son land a grilse I hooked one myself and began, confidently, to play it. Suddenly I was playing nothing. I consoled myself that this was only Monday morning. Yet by Saturday night I was empty-handed as I packed to go home.

The next year we had something of a bonanza but it was marred for me by more heart-rending losses. The river was running very high and very fast as, two early mornings running, I played fish to the steep bank then lost them as I struggled to lever them into the net. Tears before breakfast, though on the third day I was able to hail a passing bailiff from his car to save me – and the fish.

But I have gone on losing more fish than I feel I should and, of course, it has ill effects on my confidence. I start to play the fish gently, for fear of losing it, which is always fatal. When the line tightens I begin to expect to lose the fish, which has the same unwelcome effect as doubting that you are going to hit a pheasant when you raise your gun.

In Iceland in July 1988 we caught some salmon and had a marvellous time but when I hooked my best fish of the week, and had played it for five minutes, I did one of those things I really should be old enough to avoid. I looked up and shouted to my wife, 'Get the camera!' Ten seconds later, when I waded out of the water with my slack line trailing behind me, I told the gillie that I would be grateful if he would kick me.

This September I was shooting through two days of torrential rain followed by a third on which, from the moor, I could see the Findhorn falling. When the last drive finished I drove hell for leather down to the lodge, grabbed a rod and ran down to the river, tying on the fly as I went.

Sure enough, within a few minutes I was dug into a good solid fish, better than ten pounds. After a couple of minutes I felt sure that he was mine. Then the rod sprang straight and I was looking at a cast without a fly. I had botched the knot and paid the price. I walked home reciting a resolution: if I am to be a lucky fisherman I must first become a more careful one.

———————◦◦◦———————

The following stirring tale from **His Grace the Duke of Wellington** strikes a more positive note.

In 1981 I was fishing on the Moisie river in north-east Canada, as a guest of an American friend, Henry Self, who now, alas, is no longer with us. The Moisie is magnificent – 400 miles of river running, for much of its course, in two branches through the wilds of Labrador and Quebec, before joining the Gulf of St Lawrence near Sept-Iles. Henry was a member of the Moisie Salmon Club – established in the early years of this century – which had built two camps on the river, one about twenty miles upstream from the mouth, the other a further twenty miles or so north, where the river forked into east and west branches.

At dinner on the evening of 27 June members drew for the choice of pools to be fished on the following day, as was the custom of the club. Henry chose a group of pools known as the Cran Serré, about thirty miles upstream on the west branch.

The journey up to the Cran on the following day was spectacular in itself. We took off at 8 a.m. in a float-plane, flying over wooded and mountainous country with not a building to be seen until landing at the Forks Camp twenty minutes later. There we transferred to a boat for the ten-mile trip upstream. In that area the river is relatively narrow and fast and progress was slow until we negotiated our final rapid and debouched into the calmer waters of the Cran Serré.

This is a roughly circular basin about half a mile across and surrounded by high wooded hills. On the northern side the west branch comes tumbling out of a gorge over a spectacular waterfall. About 150 yards below the falls the river splits at the point of a shingle island. There are three main pools. Two, called the Premier and the Palmer, are fished from the banks on each side of the island; the third, the Mercier, is fished from the mainland.

I started by fishing the Mercier pool, using a 15-foot rod and a size 10 Munro Killer, which I had tied myself on an Esmond Drury hook. After only about a dozen casts I felt a slight knock on my fly followed, after a moment's pause, by a solid take. To begin with the fish played around fairly close to the bank and there was no indication that it was unusually large; I was thinking in terms of what I had been told was the average, about twenty pounds. After a few minutes, however, the fish took off in a tremendously powerful run upstream towards the falls, making two huge leaps, the revelation of its sheer size almost giving me heart failure. If I could land this fish it would be my biggest ever.

I was quite happy for the fish to continue to run hard upstream against the very strong current but after a dash of only eighty yards it decided to charge downstream. I was reeling frantically and had just about got on terms with the fish when he was opposite me. I hoped to play him out there as we had reached a point where I could not follow it downstream. The fish had other ideas, however, and continued steadily down until I had about 100 yards of line and backing out. There was only one thing to be done – to get into the canoe and cross to the island, where I would have more mobility.

This we did, with the fish still going down. Once on the island I ran as fast down the shingle as my wadered legs would allow and was able to recover some line, but 300 yards farther down I could see the rapids. Once the fish got into them I would almost certainly lose it – and my line.

By now I was at the bottom tip of the island with the fish a hundred yards below in strong, fast water, though definitely tiring. Desperate measures were needed. I applied more brake on the reel and began to pump the fish up, hoping the tackle would hold. Twice more it made a run for the rapids but finally I got it into shallow water and the guide got the big net under it.

The fish weighed 36 pounds and the fight had lasted thirty-five minutes – a minute per pound, which was about par for that course.

Henry and I were sharing a rod and I was glad of a rest. In no time, however, he had hooked and landed a fish of 35 pounds. I went to the upstream tip of the island and was thrilled to see hundreds of fish waiting to go up the falls. They were rolling and splashing their great broad backs on the edge of the current. Every cast produced a swirl and at my third I was into another big salmon. A tremendous fight of thirty-six minutes ensued in much the same way as the previous one. When we finally got the fish into shallow water with the net at the ready it looked to be well over thirty pounds but suddenly the line went slack. The little hook had finally straightened out and I realised that after the last fight I should have changed the fly.

While Henry fished again and caught a twenty-pounder, I changed to a size 8 Munro with a heavier hook. Within half a dozen casts I was into another fish, which felt big but did not leap like the previous two. After about twenty-five minutes of a hard, dour struggle a salmon of 34 pounds was landed.

We ate a hurried picnic lunch on the shingle, warding off the black flies which can be very tiresome, though I had the benefit of a head-net and lots of anti-fly cream. As soon as I could I was into the river again and was quickly into a fish of over twenty pounds which was lost. Henry had the same experience and it was my turn again. I hooked a lively fish which, when landed, weighed 17 pounds. Normally this would have been released but it was bleeding so much that we had to kill it. The limit was three fish, so that was it for me.

The Premier pool is only about thirty yards long. We had each been down it four times and had hooked a fish on each pass. Three of them had been over thirty pounds.

That day will remain with me as being the most exciting and memorable of the many happy days I have spent beside salmon rivers. Alas, I shall never fish that pool again. Four years ago the provincial government dispossessed the Moisie Salmon Club of its upstream water and its camp at the Forks in the interest of 'more democratic management' and handed it over to a firm of 'outfitters', whatever they may be. A sad reward for seventy years of good management.

———————————

An angler can pay a heavy price for carelessness, as **Colonel Henry Segal,** owner of the Anglers and Shooters Press and a founder member of the Theodore Gordon Flyfishers, a national organization in the United States, relates, with obvious sorrow.

I was fishing the Matapedia river, in Quebec, which is noted for big salmon. Like most Americans I fish with a single-handed 10 ½-foot graphite fly rod, which causes hilarity on big Scottish rivers but gets the fly where I want it. My last beat, at the end of a spectacular ten days which had produced one 35-pounder, was Richard's pool, one of the few which does not have to be fished from a canoe. It is a smallish pool above a waterfall and when a fish is hooked it must be played hard because if it goes over the fall the climb down is nasty.

On my tenth cast or so I hooked a really big fish – a hen salmon which leapt five times and, in spite of all I could do, went down over the fall. I released the tension on the reel to prepare for the climb down but the backing was fouled and it snapped.

It was my fault. I had loaned the rod to my daughter and had not told her of the importance of level-winding the backing. Nor had I checked it. The penalty was to lose the biggest salmon I had ever seen. The line was retrieved but the fish had broken free from it.

After tackling up with a spare spool I landed a 23-pound cock fish but even that was small recompense for the one I had lost.

———————————————

Keith Elliott, angling correspondent for *The Independent*, recalls a memorable holiday fishing trip on a Californian 'cattle boat'.

The Californians take their fishing very seriously. Unlike most places in the world, you need a permit even to dip a line into the sea, with the $46 annual charge going towards conservation and research.

Sea fishing on this coast is very big business. I was on holiday in Dana Point, just down the road from Capistrano, where the swallows come home to. It has no booksellers but five fishing shops. A few miles down the coast, a $1 million boat works solely to catch bait fish for anglers.

Travel in the other direction, to San Diego, and you can book boats for long-range fishing, spending up to three weeks and travelling more than 2,000 miles in pursuit of yellowfin tuna, wahoo, amberjack and giant sea bass.

Now the average angler carts around more than enough tackle to swamp the 44 lb baggage allowance. And when you're on holiday with the family, it's fairly difficult to persuade your wife that a big-game rod and reel, plus a box of lures and assorted tackle, are more important than, say, a change of clothes for the children.

So here I am in fish-rich waters, boats with outriggers crowding the harbour, and not a scrap of tackle. But Roy's Bait and Tackle assures me that at nearby Newport Beach, I can hire tackle and travel out in a big-game boat to fish the waters of Catalina Island, where my hero Zane Grey set records galore from the port of Avalon.

My target is not Jaws (more great white shark attacks on man on this coastline than in Australia, and all because of the burgeoning seal population, I am told). It is something less ambitious but still no slouch when it comes to a scrap – the yellowtail jack.

It is a handsome, powerful, sleek fish, looking rather like a slimmed down tuna. It averages 30 lb and accelerates faster than a Formula One car. The bait is called sardine, but these are nothing like the miserable dobs of gooey tinned things that we know. They are firm and vibrant, and the yellowtail love 'em. Or they would, if I could get my bait anywhere near the water. My first shock is that the luxury 65ft vessel is more crowded than a Vietnamese rowing boat. Every available foot (and that's about all you're allocated) is crammed with eager fishermen, fisherwomen and fisherkids. It's like a Japanese underground train and about as easy to fish in. Most of the multitude are fishing for the first time.

Of course the tangles are appalling. And they get worse when a few yellowtail are hooked, because then even the girls who work in the galley appear with fishing rods. It's easier to break your line and start again rather than trying to sort your tackle from the giant cat's cradles that develop in milli-seconds. But it simply means that you get tangled with a new set of lines. It's a great way of meeting people. Who needs singles bars?

The yellowtail wisely don't spend very long in the midst of this madness. So now it's time to head elsewhere and fish for barracuda, halibut, maybe the delicious striped or spotted bass.

And so, within shouting distance of Avalon, the real lunacy starts as the skipper, using the boat's loudspeaker, bellows at one side of the boat or the other to fish harder and haul 'em up. It is a game show for maniacs.

Can this really be the Pacific I am fishing, jammed in this mass of humanity as sabre-toothed barracuda are captured and swung dangerously past my head, while the ringmaster, a corpulent giant named Donny, flays us over a horribly efficient intercom, hidden speakers everywhere, with a wild stream of encouragement?

There's no time for rest. When it all becomes too much for me, I wind the line up and just look around in bafflement that everyone but me seems to be enjoying themselves hugely. But soon Donny spots me leaning on my shovel. He screeches, 'Hot diggety, get that guy's line in', (or some similar expression).

My hard-working neighbours look at me in disapproval. 'Come on, join our tangle,' they seem to say. One of the few crew who is not fishing himself baits the hook and I'm off again. Why don't the fish keep miles away from this floating asylum? But my line has scarcely hit the water before a 10 lb barracuda shoots up to grab the sardine. I try to pull the bait clear but I'm too late. Another tangle. How do the Americans stay so calm about it? Ugly brown pelicans, attracted by the noise and the sardines which come of the hook, float around disdainfully. At least they can stop fishing when they want.

Thank God I didn't book for the full day trip. This is merely the three-quarter day special, but it still runs from 5 a.m. to 4 p.m. And it seems like twice as long as the California sun pounds down on this seething, feverish horde of demented beings. For me, used to boats where six is a crowd, it is a nightmare. I now know why those in the know call these 'cattle boats' and keep well clear of them.

I don't think time has ever gone so slowly on a fishing trip. But mercifully it comes to an end. The captor of the biggest yellowtail, a grizzled old man straight out of Hemingway, right down to the straw hat, collects $150 for the biggest yellowtail. Photos are taken, fish cleaned (even my miserable collection) and the ringmaster heads the circus back to town.

On the way he says: 'Hey you guys, we've still got 25 places for tonight's twilight trip, so get in quick.'

I don't ask what twilight fishing means. It probably means doing it all over again, but in the dark. I think I would rather splash around in the sea and pretend I'm a seal.

———————◦◦———————

His Grace the Duke of Atholl is not a keen or practised fisherman but he has had his moment of glory.

Unfortunately I am not a fisherman of any skill but I did, for some time, hold the record for the largest trout caught on my stepfather's 'put and take' loch at Ardchatten in Argyllshire. It was a monster of 8 pounds 5 ounces.

I was not very popular either with him or with his more proficient guests at this piece of total luck.

I thoroughly enjoyed catching it and was looking forward to eating it but I had no chance. He gave it for the centrepiece at the harvest festival!

———————◦◦———————

Alan Lawrence, landlord of the Fox and Hounds Inn near Pontefract, recalls a similar moment of disappointment.

A friend of mine called Joe Taylor, who was new to salmon fishing, was trying his hand on the Carnock beat of the Eden, in Cumbria. Fishing from a boat, which is not the easiest way to start, he had appalling trouble with over-runs and other problems. To his astonishment, and even more to the gillie's who was rowing, he hooked a sizeable fish and after a very protracted struggle, since he was so terrified of losing it, it was landed into the boat.

It was the only fish he hooked that day and as the boat was being rowed to the shore he picked up the salmon, laid it on one of the seats and began to tell the gillie what he was going to do with the fish, as he ogled it. With his finger he divided it into several slices saying, 'I'm going to give that cut to my mother, keep that one, give that one to my sister and the tail is for my brother.'

As the boat struck the bank the gillie suggested that Joe should get out with his rod and that he would bring the fish. But Joe was not to be parted from his prize. 'No. You bring the rod. I'm taking the fish.' Being unused to boats, he slipped as he tried to clamber out and the salmon, with all its lovingly sliced prime cuts, disappeared forever into the depths of the Eden.

———————◦————————

It was with immense sadness that I learned of the sudden death of **Ken Robinson**, the fishing manager of the Inchmarlo beat of the Dee, and I record his account of his most memorable evening as a tribute to a delightful riverside companion and a fisherman of superlative skill, whose Spey-casting, in particular, was a wonder to watch.

There is no time that I enjoy fishing more than during the darkening, that brief period, exaggerated in northern areas like Scotland, between the onset of twilight and the night. For reasons I do not understand, salmon which have been dour all day will suddenly become active and, just as quickly, sink back into repose. Living as I now do right on the north bank of the Dee on the Inchmarlo beat, overlooking the river, I have enjoyed fine sport in the darkening many times but none quite like the experience on a certain mid-April evening after a day when, with the river in flood, all the rods were blank.

The river had been falling from lunch time and, though I told the guests that fishing should improve, they were committed to a dinner and asked me to fish for them. I had the whole beat to myself.

Inchmarlo has thirteen named pools in a mile of water but there would be no time to move about. I chose the Fawn, a short pool which is equipped with a concrete walkway, reached by a wooden bridge. The water was running a foot over the walkway, which is only a foot wide, with gaps in it, so fishing down it had its hazards. As the pool takes only half an hour to fish I decided to begin at 8.15 pm.

As soon as the full length of line was fishing my size 8 fly – an unweighted 1 ¼-inch tube, sparsely dressed and mainly black – I felt that lovely long pull of a fish taking and was in business. To land a fish there it is necessary to return to the bank so I gingerly retraced my steps through the swirling water, safely negotiating the gaps in the walkway. My wife, Phyllis, who had followed me on her evening walk, was nicely placed to net a fresh ten-pounder. It was the first fish of the week, with time enough for another. The next one duly obliged and while my wife continued her walk upstream I hooked and landed two more. She was back in time to net the fifth, hooked in the tail of the pool.

We were home in time to hear the nine o'clock television news with two fish of 9 pounds, one of 10 and two of 11, one taken on the first cast, one on the last, and all fresh. All in about forty minutes' fishing! It had never happened to me before in fifty years. I doubt that it will ever happen again but in the wonderful sport of salmon fishing anything is possible.

The following experience, contributed by **Major-General Sir John Acland,** was so near to being a most unusual feat that it is well worthy of permanent record.

I was fishing the Test on a beat where various stocking experiments had been tried. In the course of the afternoon, fishing a small spent gnat, I caught three trout – a wild brown, a rainbow and a Canadian brook trout – all around the two-pound mark. Shortly after the last my fly was taken, ferociously, in a bit of fast water and I thought I was into something really big. When it came to the net, however, I could see it was a fish of only 1 ½ pounds but was a sea trout.

The river keeper was as surprised as I was to see the sea trout. 'What a triumph it would be,' I said 'to get a salmon, which would make five different salmonids in the same day on one beat of the Test!'

It was an idle remark but the keeper took it seriously. 'This morning there was a salmon lying just below the bridge at the bottom of the beat,' be said enthusiastically. 'But, remember, it's dry-fly upstream at all times!'

Down to the bridge I went and there, sure enough, was a salmon of seven or eight pounds, lying in about four feet of water below it. With trembling hands I tied on a larger fly, a yellow partridge. After the third cast from about ten yards below him I thought the fish moved a little. Two casts later he took it. Even as he did so, the thought suddenly struck me that, in my excitement, I had not changed my cast and was still fishing with 5x! Disaster stared me in the face and was not long in coming. The salmon broke me as he ran up under the bridge.

I sat, disconsolate, on the bank, knowing that I would never get such an opportunity again. I never have and wonder whether anyone ever had before.

For **Mr Shirley E. Woods**, the well known Canadian angler and writer, the dry fly brought salmon aplenty, including a much-appreciated bonus fish.

Dry-fly fishing is my favourite method of angling, and the Atlantic salmon is my favourite quarry. For years my ambition was to hook and land a 25-pound salmon on a dry fly.

This proved a frustrating quest because relatively few rivers hold large salmon, and when you locate a big fish the conditions must be just right. As the seasons passed I became increasingly obsessed with my goal. Roaming from river to river I had some fleeting opportunities – but I botched them all.

In 1979, through a stroke of luck I managed to book a week at the end of June as a paying guest on the York river. The York, located in the Canadian Gaspé, is renowned both for the size of its salmon and their willingness to take a dry fly.

The York Club owned eighteen miles of river. That week, three of us had the entire stretch all to ourselves. It was just as well for 1979 was a lean year, and many of the pools were barren.

Each angler was assigned two guides; mine were Cecil Eden and Terry Miller. Cecil, the stern man or senior guide, was a spry little man of seventy-six who knew every stone and riffle in the river and, I suspect, every salmon by its first name. Both he and Terry, the husky young bow man, were good-natured and courteous. When I told them I intended to fish the dry fly exclusively (a method considered much less efficient than the wet fly) they accepted the news with equanimity.

On Monday, the first day, I lost a good-sized fish that wrapped the leader around a boulder in the rapids.

On Tuesday we went to a gin-clear pool called the Tub. Near the tail we saw two salmon lying side by side; one was over twenty pounds, the other half that size. To avoid spooking them I had to wade well above them and cast a long line. After an hour, the smaller salmon took the dry fly with a great splash and was subsequently released. The commotion, however, drove the big fish from his lie and that was that.

Wednesday, at Spruins, I came close to realising my dream. Spruins is a narrow rock-bound pool, shaped like a dog's leg, which empties into a heavy rapid. Salmon lie in all three sections of the pool and, when the light is right, can be clearly seen swaying in the currents. It is a superb place for the dry fly.

That day the fish were in a taking mood, and I hooked four. The first pulled free in the rapids after a brief struggle. The second (estimated by Cecil to be thirty pounds) I had on for half an hour. The end came when it headed for the rapids, and I tried to stop it. The leader hummed with the strain, then snapped.

The loss of this fish devastated my morale. Killing a 20-pounder and a 22-pounder that afternoon would, under normal circumstances, have delighted me, but back at camp that night I was haunted by the memory of the big one that got away.

On Thursday morning there was only one small fish of about ten pounds in the Tub. It took some coaxing, but eventually inhaled the dry fly. After a short fight Cecil netted and released it. In the afternoon, at Spruins, I stalked a good salmon that rose three times before seizing the fly. A few minutes later, for no apparent reason, the hook pulled free. Cecil said that fish would certainly have weighed twenty-five pounds.

I was leaving after lunch on Saturday, so Friday was my last full day on the river. Gloomily, I reflected that I had had some wonderful chances to take a big fish on the dry fly, but now time was running out.

Friday morning we fished several pools from the canoe without success. That evening, when the sun was off the water, we tried Spruins.

Shortly after we arrived I was fast to a large and determined fish. It shot upstream, jumped twice, sulked behind a boulder, surged downstream, lanced out of the water again, and displayed a full repertoire of tricks. Running along the rocky shore I did my best to keep up with it, expecting at any moment to feel the line go slack. Then, after a pause to gather its strength, the salmon bolted for the rapids. With foreboding, and a sense of *déjà vu*, I knew I must hold it in the pool. At first it seemed hopeless, but by pumping and reeling I slowly regained my backing.

After what seemed like ages, I saw the end of my fly line on the spool.

Cecil eased into the water with his net and stood motionless as a heron. Carefully I swung the rod tip into the shore and the fish turned towards him. All of us held our breath. With a quick thrust Cecil deftly scooped the fish into the net. The salmon thrashed violently, and for a moment I feared the old guide would be dragged into the river. But seconds later he had it safe on the beach. It was a lovely fresh-run hen, bright as a new-minted coin – and it weighed 26 pounds.

To everyone's relief, I had finally realised my ambition.

Walking down the forest trail to Spruins on the last morning I was at peace with the world. No longer driven by the desire to achieve, I intended to enjoy myself. When we reached the pool I told my guides that if we were lucky enough to take a fish we would release it. What I hoped to capture were some good photos.

Rather than wading, I stood on the granite wall of the upper channel and cast across the pool. With the sun over my shoulder I could see the torpedo shapes of numerous salmon lying along the ledges. That morning I rolled five different fish while Terry photographed their head-and-tail rises with my camera. One salmon was on briefly but as soon as it felt the steel it threw the bulky dry fly, which sailed over the water like a wounded sparrow. I reacted to our abrupt parting with an uncharacteristic 'Bravo!'

Just before it was time to leave, I hooked a very big fish. Because salmon that are to be released should be played quickly, I really put the butt to this one as it careened around the pool. Within fifteen minutes, it was positioned below me, ready for the net. Rather than have old Cecil risk his neck clambering down the steep rock face, I asked Terry to do the netting. Cecil objected, but was mollified when I explained that this was an ideal opportunity for Terry to get some practice.

On his first attempt, Terry hoisted the salmon half out of the water and then allowed it to flop back into the river.

My rod bucked wildly, the reel screamed, and I was sure I'd lost it – but I didn't care. Miraculously, the fish stayed on, and by taking liberties with my tackle I swiftly winched it back into position. This time Terry made no mistake and the salmon was securely trapped in the net.

Terry should then have removed the hook and slipped the fish back into the water. Instead, he and Cecil pleaded with me to keep it, adding that neither of them had eaten fresh salmon that year. I vacillated for a moment, and then reluctantly agreed to their request. After admiring the salmon, which was a beauty, I turned away to dismantle my rod. Meanwhile, Cecil and Terry set about weighing our trophy. Snapping the lid of my fly box shut, I looked up and asked them, 'How much?'

Cecil peered at the scales intently.

'Sir, this fish you wanted to release weighs 31 pounds!'

Such determination and skill is also very much in evidence in the following story from **Tony Pawson**, the former World Fly-fishing Champion.

The thousands of lakes and rivers in Tasmania teem with wild brown trout which are descendants of a remarkable shipment of trout ova from the Test, Itchen, Wick and Wey in 1864. Rainbows have been added in many waters but, throughout the territory, which is very beautiful when the sun shines and the water sparkles, the policy is to assist natural breeding rather than stock with hatchery fish. Rare exceptions are the giant "triploid" rainbows being stocked in selected waters. These were known to the locals as "steroid" trout but after the Seoul Olympics they have been rechristened "Ben Johnsons".

My first experience of Tasmanian fishing was when I attended the Australian Freshwater Assembly to which I had been invited so that Australia might consider entering the World Fly-fishing Championship in England in 1987. This they did with some success, their team of five beating nineteen other countries to finish runners-up behind England. Thus encouraged, Australia applied for and was granted the right to stage the event the following year as part of the bicentennial celebrations.

With sixteen countries competing, the event was staged on three Tasmanian lakes – the delightful London Lakes. These are some of the few privately owned waters which specialise in large trout cruising the margins in the early dawn. The 6-hour fishing sessions on one lake therefore began at 5.30 am. The lake called Little Pine is noted for large hatches of duns so the sessions there were timed to finish at 4 pm, while in Bronte Lagoon they ended at 8.30 pm to allow the evening rise to be included.

While I was there on my first trip on the Great Lakes Jim Allen, one of Tasmania's top fly-fishers, went "polaroiding", i.e. wading in the shallow water, spotting a large trout and flicking a Red Tag or nymph in front of it. The cast needs to be careful and accurate, because the fish are easily spooked, but Jim returned to the hotel with four trout weighing almost 40 pounds! However, to the good fortune of our England team, the weather was so wet and wild during the World Championship that the delicate skills of "polaroiding" proved no match for working the dropper in the wind, wading far from the shore and fishing with unbroken concentration for six hours, whatever the weather. In those conditions the England team had another comfortable win.

My main interest was concentrated on my son, the youngest of the English team. He relished the conditions, commenting 'This is home from home. Just like Rutland Water in April in a Force 8.' Only the English team caught well on Little Pine until the Australian, Terry Piggott, switched to our method after four fruitless hours. The pleasure of then catching well enough to finish third in the individual event was tempered by having to admit to fishing the "Pommie" way.

The weather relented a little on the final day of the 3-day event but remained so chilly, on what was the official opening of summer, that one of the England team remarked 'The only rise to which I cast throughout the event turned out to be a platypus which looked as if it was nymphing.'

By the time my son John, and Brian Thomas of England had caught five each in the last session at Bronte, it was clear that one or the other would win the individual championship by a wide margin. At that point my son hooked and lost five trout in succession, the last one of about six pounds just as he was about to slide the net under it. However, in the last half hour he landed three, the last one, which won him the championship, with only one minute of the eighteen hour event left! All his last five fish were taken on his own Bibio pattern – exactly the same as the one on which I took most of my fish when winning the championship four years earlier on the Tormes River in Spain.

When anglers remember a particular salmon they are usually able to recall the name of the pool in which they encountered it. In fact, salmon pools become old friends and their names, which sometimes go back for centuries, are an endless source of pleasure. Some names are also a sense of wonderment. Why, for example, is the name Floating Bank so common on so many beats of so many rivers? Recently I made it my business to find out and the result was fascinating. Before the days of tractors and trucks the timber felled by the riverside on each estate was floated downstream to a collecting point, as it still is in Canada, for example. For this purpose it had first to be pulled to a convenient bank, usually with an incline and some space behind it and with a convenient riverside track. That particular place was called the Floating Bank and the name lingers on.

In most cases the origin of a salmon pool's name is lost way back in time, but there is one I know with a modern name which is equally unforgettable....

For several years my husband and I had the pleasure of fishing the river Wye, at Ross-on-Wye, through the kindness of our friend, the late Sir Charles Clore, who owned the water, which had once belonged to Guy's Hospital. The gillie there was a very able fisherman rather aptly named Moody.

There was one pool which had a most unusual name – The Lavatory – not, as might be expected, due to its being a pollution point but because in previous years there had been a privy there for the use of anglers. It was a good pool with fairly fast water which could be fished from both sides – a rather pleasant change from the other canal-like pools set between steep clay banks.

For that reason, but also because it had produced some good salmon, it was my husband's favourite. I thought that Moody might have put it less ambiguously when, sensing my husband's boredom with the clay banks, he shouted in a loud voice across the river, rather near a main road, 'Mr Chapman Pincher looks as though he wants to go to the Lavatory.'

However, it was easy to slip into the habit because, on a later occasion when my husband's gaff had slipped down a steep bank into deep water, he explained to Moody that he had 'lost it in the Lavatory', which would have sounded quite extraordinary to a stranger.

Many women would liked to have a rose named after them. I would prefer a salmon pool or, perhaps, better still, a salmon fly. Neither is likely but one of my kind contributors, **Boy Pilkington**, of the glass family, has sent me an entertaining account of how a new and highly successful salmon fly came to be named.

I had the good fortune to be one of a party of five rods fishing the lower Oykel in May 1954, when we broke the existing record for the river – 203 fish in a fortnight, the best being 21 pounds, a fresh fish which, luckily, took my fly. The fishing was then owned by Lady Ross, widow of Sir Charles Ross of Balnagowan, and when she heard of our good fortune she left a bottle of whisky for us on the hall table. It was labelled 'Glen Oykel Pure Malt Whisky, especially distilled for Sir Charles Ross of Balnagowan'. I christened our bottle 'Old Charlie'. It was powerful stuff; when my cousin flung the dregs of his glass into the fire he nearly blew the place up.

Flushed by success, I decided to invent a fly and call it 'Old Charlie'. The dressing was to have a suitably alcoholic theme, as follows:

Tail - golden pheasant topping (Chateau Yquem)
Body - wine-coloured floss silk (Taylor's '27 port)
Ribbing - gold tinsel (Veuve Cliquot Champagne)
Hackle - dried apricot cock's hackle (apricot brandy)
Wing - deer Hair (Grand Marnier)
Sides - jungle cock (Black and White whisky)
Head - scarlet sealing wax (Pedlar's sloe gin)

'Old Charlie' proved to be highly successful and is much used on the Oykel, Helmsdale, Brora and northern rivers.

In July 1988 I was lucky enough to be fishing the Oykel again when a new record was established – 210 fish to twelve rods in six days. Out of the nineteen which I caught Old Charlie accounted for all but two, and he also connected for some of the other rods.

I might have some slight claim regarding the name of one pool – on the River Driva in Norway – because I discovered a lie there which nobody else seemed to know about and which almost always produced a big fish. It was also the scene of my rather original method of dealing with a beached salmon.

On a visit to the Driva with my husband I was left in a safe but, I thought, unpromising pool, having been briefly instructed on the art of beaching a salmon, which I had never done before. Within ten minutes of being left alone I hooked a large fish, played it to exhaustion and walked backwards to bring it over the shallows to the beaching point. When it was almost there the bait came out of its mouth and the fish began flopping back into deeper water. I dropped the rod, ran to the fish and, since it was too big for me to grasp, sat on it. Seizing a stone from the bottom I then managed to dispatch the fish.

Having recovered my breath and not having shipped too much water into my waist waders, I hauled the salmon out and hid it on the bank, covered with leaves. The others who had enjoyed the benefit of boats and gillies returned blank and having seen no sign of any fish on my bank were not prepared to believe me when, having put my rod on the transport, I asked them to wait while I went for my salmon. It weighed 24 pounds.

My sitting-on-the-fish technique was used in even more exciting – and certainly more dangerous – circumstances in a situation described to me, in typically graphic language, by my old friend **Professor Harry Messel** of Sydney University, who is a one-off character if ever there was one. The quarry was not exactly a fish but, as fishing tackle was used, I feel justified in including the story here.

Professor Messel had been researching the habits of the Australian salt-water crocodile (*Crocodylus porosus*), which inhabits remote inlets and tidal rivers in Northern Australia, with a view to conserving this largest living reptile and contemporary of the dinosaurs. These crocodiles are fast movers, aggressive, and, since they can reach a length of twenty feet, extremely dangerous. Attempts to use drugged darts to capture them live for weighing, marking and release had proved impracticable because the animals so often drowned. The only practicable technique was to cruise in a dinghy in the dark using a spotlight which was reflected from the crocs' eyes. A small harpoon, which latched into the scaly skin and was attached to a handline on a large fishing reel, was then thrown at the croc from close range. The croc then had to be 'played' to the side of the dinghy, where a noose was slipped over its jaws and it was hauled into the boat.

The Prof had harpooned an eight-footer and it fought so strongly in shallow water that almost all the line was out. After a terrific and spectacular ten-minute fight, with the croc repeatedly trying to attack the boat with its teeth, it was hauled into the boat. It thrashed around as no other croc had ever done before and there was real fear that one or more of the three people aboard would be badly bitten. In desperation the Professor shouted to the heaviest man, 'For God's sake sit on it!' With great courage – he was very frightened – he did so and the croc was subdued.

As Professor Messel says, 'Any sane person would agree that an academic who banishes himself from comfort and civilization to grab crocodiles must be mad.'

While also not quite a fish, another aquatic creature imprinted itself so indelibly on my memory that I have taken the liberty of including its true story.

I am no expert with a prawn but I have had occasion to try to induce an aquatic creature to take one. The story has international overtones.

There is an airstrip close to Diani Beach, near Mombasa, from which our friend the late Bruce McKenzie used to fly a four-seater plane. After a wonderful safari holiday,

I was saying farewell there to his wife and her two small boys when I was given a small bag as a parting present. It contained a collection of small shells, which they had made on the beach as the tide had ebbed that morning. I stowed it in my hand luggage and Bruce ferried us to Nairobi – the last time he would do so because, not long afterwards, he was assassinated in just such an airplane by a bomb planted at the instigation of Idi Amin.

On arrival home in Surrey I put all the small shells into a large open shell, from a previous trip, which I kept on my dressing table. Several days passed before I noticed that one shell was on the floor. I put it back and, to my surprise, it was on the floor again the following day. On closer inspection I saw a row of small pink claws tucked into the opening and realised I had a live hermit crab.

As I was to dine with my husband that evening at a restaurant in London I put Peter the Hermit, as I called my new diminutive friend, into a matchbox, pierced with a few holes for air, and placed it in my handbag.

While we were enjoying aperitifs and ordering the meal at the Écu de France, I remembered Peter and said to the waiter, 'Please bring me one small prawn on a plate along with my soup.' The waiter, an old friend, looked puzzled, but, being very professional, made no comment.

When the prawn arrived I put the shell on the table and to the waiter's astonishment it ran, at speed, to the edge, where my husband caught it. The prawn was not a success and, as I discovered later, the only flesh Peter would eat had to be uncooked and rotten. We had stinking fish on the radiator for days.

The McKenzies lived near us when they were in England and I called to see them just before Bruce, then an aide to the President, Jomo Kenyatta, was due to take off for Nairobi. I asked him if he would do Peter and myself a kindness by returning him and his shell to Diani Beach. The project appealed to his sense of humour and, with great laughter, he put the matchbox in his brief-case. He was flying back with the Kenyan Attorney-General, Charles

Njonjo, and on the journey they decided that the return of such a distinguished Kenyan as Peter merited a ceremony.

In due course, both men flew to Diani Beach, where, in the shade of a famous baobab tree, they met up with a certain Colonel Colquhoun Colquhoun, a local person of some importance. The three then marched to the beach and in a solemn act of repatriation placed Peter in a rock-pool, in which, recognising home territory, he was soon moving about.

The following day a cable arrived for me jointly from Bruce McKenzie, Charles Njonjo and Colonel Colquhoun Colquhoun announcing: 'Operation Hermit Crab completed.'

In view of the persons involved, the intelligence authorities may still be pondering over the significance of this secret 'operation' if they intercepted the cable, as they probably did.

———◦———

Another memorable marine experience involving something that was not quite a fish befell my friend **Peter Hutley**. It is described by his wife Ann, who witnessed the battle.

It took place one stormy afternoon between the Straits of Bonifacio, between Corsica and Sardinia, in our marvellous old boat, the ketch *Mollymawk* built in 1899, and the home of our family and friends for over thirty years. We thought the time had come for big game fishing and the installation of a 'fighting chair', though no one had heard of this sport in the putrid waters of the Mediterranean, except for our skipper, Alfredo, a former commercial fisherman. Without Alfredo's ration of wine he would not take to sea at all – 'Petrol for Alfie' we used to cry before leaving land. Then, well stoked up, he would chug us to the next port, where we would take our children to the nearest bar – snooker was learned at an early age. Our summers were filled with stories of big fish he had caught – always on the day after we had departed for the airport.

So game fishing it was to be. Bait was put out as we left the shores of Sardinia for Corsica, always a dangerous crossing without a strong engine. All was well until 'zing zing' and the line flew out from my husband Peter's rod. Alfredo was right after all! I rushed below for the ciné-camera and the rest gathered round. Peter was in the fighting chair, an old deckchair harnessed up with the trappings needed to play big fish.

Alfredo smiled, knowingly. 'Marlin, marlin' he muttered in his broken English. 'Biggerda fishka' – and we breathed in his words.

'Big tuna, I imagine,' Peter said, screwing up his eyes to trace the course of the humming line stretched out from his doubled-up rod. He instructed me to keep the camera firmly trained on him while the good ship, *Mollymawk*, was throttled down to fight the fish. It was my first experience of the tense excitement and overwhelming anticipation that fishermen experience.

It was fine for the first hour or two. Then the children began to get bored and it was long past tea-time. Charts were forgotten as Alfredo's sparkling eyes were trained on the line which ebbed and flowed as the boat rolled and tossed and the sun began to go down.

'It sometimes takes nine hours with a really big fish.' I remember telling Peter. 'I have seen those Americans of Florida, burnt and wasted by the time they got their fish in.' I recalled that people playing big fish are not supposed to be given help and rushed down to the chart room to consult Hemingway on the subject.

Peter was grimly determined to hang on, however long it took, winding in the reel when he could.

Dusk was upon us and we had a long way to go. Only Alfredo remained undaunted. Feeling sick with the constant rolling and the harness rubbing into his shoulders and stomach, Peter suddenly shouted 'It's coming, it's coming!' and we all rushed to the side. There was no net big enough and all we had was a blunt boat hook. Nevertheless we stood by for imminent action.

As the enormous plastic bag rose out of the water, filled with Italian trash from the beaches, a sudden silence fell upon our crew. The children looked at Alfredo with accusing eyes. Peter said nothing beyond commanding a large gin and tonic. Alfredo made himself scarce by going down for another top-up of his vino.

That night, in the darkened snooker bar of an Italian village, the children recounted to us the vision of Alfredo telling his friends the story of the huge fish which got away, after eight hours struggle in the dangerous waters of the Straits of Bonifacio.

———————————⊶⊷———————————

In an unusually adventurous life **Alan Bristow**, of helicopter fame, has done most things and when I asked him for a fishing experience he produced a story which, while not quite about a fish, was so riveting that I cannot resist including it.

Shortly after the Second World War, Alan founded a small company, Air Whaling Ltd, to exploit the use of the helicopter in spotting whales for Antarctic whaling vessels and to assist ships to find their way out of pack ice when no ice-breaker was available. To his great surprise he discovered that whales are virtually both deaf and blind to what is going on in the air. He could approach and hover fifty feet above a group of whales in a Westland 55 Whirlwind and they would take no notice. Tests with sticks of dynamite dropped by parachute and exploded a few feet above the whales did not appear to trouble them. They detected a helicopter at lower heights but only because of the pressure which the down-draught then exerted on them.

The obvious question posed itself — could helicopters be

used instead of ships for hunting whales? There was one obvious advantage to the whale populations if this was feasible – a lactating whale with a young calf could easily be spotted in the clear Antarctic waters from a helicopter and could be spared. Such whales were often harpooned by ships which could not see a calf.

Alan Bristow and his few colleagues therefore returned to Britain to undertake the necessary research and development in Portland Bay. They needed a light-weight harpoon which could be fired from a recoilless gun fitted in a Whirlwind and would hit a 2-foot-diameter target from a distance of about a hundred yards. This problem was solved in collaboration with Colonel Blacker, who had been involved in developing recoilless weapons during the war and held a patent, which he sold.

The harpoon was linked to the aircraft by a thin cable which contained a wire capable of conducting an electric shock severe enough to kill a large blue whale instantaneously. The shock was provided by a generator carried in the helicopter.

The harpoon also contained a capsule of liquid which, on impact, generated enough gas to inflate the dead whale and ensure that it would float. It was also possible to pump air through from a compressor.

Obviously, the cable had to be fitted with a weak link in case the whale was not killed and dived. Without that, it could have taken the helicopter with it.

The team then devised a simple gunsight and after six months of tests against drums towed behind a launch Alan was certain that they could kill the biggest whale, instantaneously and humanely, and that their equipment and services would be in big demand.

Out of the blue in 1953 representatives of a Dutch whaling company, who had heard of the experiments, asked for a demonstration. They were so impressed that they offered Air Whaling £1 million for all the patents.

With what turned out to be brilliant foresight, Alan accepted. He was told to turn up at a City office with two suitcases, which were then filled with £1 million in English banknotes.

It was Alan's first million and he ploughed it all into Air Whaling, changing the name to Bristow Helicopters, which was to become the biggest helicopter-operating company in the world.

Four months later, the International Whaling Commission, having also got wind of the developments, banned any killing of whales from the air. That ban still remains.

John Sautelle found that a helicopter without a harpoon was equally effective.

A friend called Ian Sarginson, who owned a property in the South Island of New Zealand, and who was every bit as keen an angler as myself, took me up in his small helicopter to an Alpine lake about 4,000 feet high. He had assured me that there were plenty of trout there but that they refused to take a fly. He had taken his family camping there for several days and while the children caught plenty of trout on spinners, Ian, for all his skill and experience, had been totally unable to interest the fish in any kind of fly, fished wet or dry.

I was so keen to get started and prove him wrong that I assembled my rod before we set off, with the two pieces apart, and a dry Royal Wulff, a favourite of mine, on the cast. The sight of the smallish glacier-fed lake was glorious as we approached and Ian set the machine down about twenty yards from the shore. I had the door open the moment we touched down and by the time I had sprinted to the water's edge I had joined the two pieces of the rod together and was all set to cast.

To my surprise, a brown trout of about five pounds was cruising along the bank below me obviously slurping floating insects. With a short side-cast I put the Royal Wulff just in front of it and the fish took it immediately. It had all happened so quickly that on looking round I saw that the rotor blades were still turning and was greeted by Ian with an inevitable 'You old bastard!'

And lastly, a story from **Barbara Hawkins** which may serve as a gentle reminder to any angler who considers reneging on a promise made in friendship!

In time past a friend of mine called Steve Player was a whipper-in to 'the well-known Master of Foxhounds, Maurice Kingscote. Despite their age difference they became great friends, often dining together. On one such evening when the port had gone round several times the conversation turned to funerals, about which Maurice had something of a fixation. He would attend funerals anywhere, treating them as a social occasion to be enjoyed. It was no surprise to Steve that, being considerably older, he should bring up the question of his own funeral and insisted that, when his time came, Steve should be there. Assuring Maurice that the event must still be far in the future, he promised to attend, if still in the land of the living himself. Maurice made it clear that he set much store by the promise and would be deeply upset in the nether world if it was not kept.

In the following spring, when Steve was on his annual visit to fish the Naver, way up in the Scottish Highlands, his wife telephoned him with the sad news that Maurice had been killed in a car crash and that the funeral was to be two days later.

It was half-way through the week and with the road journey taking so long then, there would have been no time to return to fish so, perhaps understandably, Steve decided to remain and to be represented at the funeral by a friend.

The next day everything seemed to go wrong and Steve put this down, partly at least, to his grief. On the day of the funeral it was his turn to fish his favourite pool, called the Skail, a somewhat eerie, dark stretch with deep water running under a rocky bank on the far side. He fished a little way down the pool, totally engrossed in his casting, when he experienced a strong feeling that he was being watched. He looked all around and finally spotted a big, grey dog fox sitting on a rock on the other side, staring at him.

He pointed the fox out to the gillie and they shouted to make him move but, instead of loping away, it moved closer up the side of the pool and sat on the bank only some fifteen yards away. There, unlike any normal wild fox, it continued to sit and stare fixedly at the fisherman until at last it climbed to the sky-line where it cocked its leg, contemptuously, in Steve's direction before vanishing.

The gillie's assurance that, in all his years on the beat, he had never seen a fox there before, hardened the suspicion in Steve's mind that he was not the only one being represented during the funeral. Indeed, he felt so guilty that he stopped fishing for the day and, I understand, could never bring himself to fish that pool again.

Since then, I have often fished Skail myself, but never without scanning the rocky bank for the sight of that old dog fox.